Assessing Critical Thinking in Elementary Schools

Meeting the Common Core

Rebecca Stobaugh

EYE ON EDUCATION
6 DEPOT WAY WEST, SUITE 106
LARCHMONT, NY 10538
(914) 833–0551
(914) 833–0761 fax
www.eyeoneducation.com

Library of Congress Cataloging-in-Publication Data

Stobaugh, Rebecca.
  Assessing critical thinking in elementary schools : meeting the
common core / Rebecca Stobaugh.
        pages cm
  Includes bibliographical references.
  ISBN 978-1-59667-236-9
1. Critical thinking--Study and teaching (Elementary) I. Title.
  LB1590.3.S786 2013
  370.15'2--dc23

                                                      2012049504

10 9 8 7 6 5 4 3 2 1

Sponsoring Editors: Robert Sickles and Lauren Davis
Copyeditor: Laurie Lieb
Designer and Compositor: Rick Soldin
Cover Designer: Dave Strauss, 3FoldDesign

Also Available from Eye On Education

**Assessing Critical Thinking in Middle and High Schools:
Meeting the Common Core**
Rebecca Stobaugh

Rigor Is NOT a Four-Letter Word, Second Edition
Barbara R. Blackburn

**Critical Thinking and Formative Assessments:
Increasing the Rigor in Your Classroom**
Betsy Moore and Todd Stanley

Rigor Made Easy: Getting Started
Barbara R. Blackburn

**Rigor in Your School:
A Toolkit for Leaders**
Ronald Williamson and Barbara R. Blackburn

**Rigorous Schools and Classrooms:
Leading the Way**
Ronald Williamson and Barbara R. Blackburn

**Teacher-Made Assessments:
How to Connect Curriculum, Instruction, and Student Learning**
Christopher R. Gareis and Leslie W. Grant

**Differentiated Assessment for
Middle and High School Classrooms**
Deborah Blaz

**Handbook on Differentiated Instruction
for Middle and High Schools**
Sheryn Spencer Northey

**Differentiating Assessment in Middle and High School:
Mathematics and Science**
Sheryn Spencer Waterman

**Differentiating Assessment in Middle and High School:
English and Social Studies**
Sheryn Spencer Waterman

**Formative Assessment for English Language Arts:
A Guide for Middle and High School Teachers**
Amy Benjamin

This book is dedicated to my children.
May they always challenge themselves to reach their full potential.

Supplemental Downloads

The implementation tools and discussion questions in this book are also available on Eye On Education's website as Adobe Acrobat files. Permission has been granted to purchasers of this book to download these resources and print them.

You can access these downloads by visiting Eye On Education's website: www.eyeoneducation.com. From the home page, click on FREE, then click on Supplemental Downloads. Alternatively, you can search or browse our website to find this book, then click on "Log in to Access Supplemental Downloads."

Your book-buyer access code is **AES-7236-9.**

Index of Supplemental Downloads

Contents

Acknowledgments

Several teacher candidates and current teachers partnered with me to develop the assessments in this text: Amanda F. Cook, Samantha McMahan, Alicia DiTommaso, Bradley Boaz, Aaron Young, Shelby Overstreet, Adam Spinks, and Kacey Page. Kristy Cartwright also provided critical support in editing. Janet Tassell and Martha Day have previously collaborated with me in presenting and publishing on this topic. Finally, I am thankful to my husband as well as my parents, who have always supported my aspirations.

Meet the Author

Rebecca Stobaugh has been a principal and middle and high school teacher. While serving as a teacher, she was named Social Studies Teacher of the Year by the Kentucky Council for Social Studies in 2004. In her position as a middle school principal, she focused on aligning curriculum, increasing the level of critical thinking in assessments and instruction, and establishing a school-wide discipline plan. She is the author of *Assessing Critical Thinking in Middle and High Schools*. She received a PhD from the University of Louisville. Currently, she serves as an assistant professor at Western Kentucky University, teaching assessment and unit-planning courses in the teacher education program. She supervises first-year teachers and consults with school districts on critical thinking, instructional strategies, assessment, technology integration, and other topics.

Introduction: Engaging in Critical Thinking

Many complex problems in life demand critical thinking to examine the situation and formulate a solution. Whether it is a problem with your car, your neighbor, or your job, memorized terms do not prepare you for these situations. In order to be primed for these life experiences, students need experience engaging in higher-level thinking tasks and assessments.

Critical thinking skills should be infused into daily instruction in order to adequately prepare students for school assessments, rigorous college expectations, employers' demands, and complex life situations. Equipping students with critical thinking skills enables students to reason effectively, make rational judgments and decisions, and solve problems.

Since there are many misconceptions about levels of thinking, this book initially delves deeply into the revised Bloom's cognitive taxonomy to build greater understanding of each level. Next, prevailing misconceptions about critical thinking and problems associated with designing high-level thinking tasks and assessments will be addressed. A solution will then be provided to increase the level of critical thinking in instructional tasks and assessments—using interpretive exercises. The three successive chapters demonstrate how to incorporate interpretive exercises using scenarios, visuals, and quotes. Finally, the book will share ideas on how to establish a culture of thinking in a classroom along with techniques to include interpretive exercises into instruction and assessments. At the end of each chapter are discussion questions, practical applications, and supplementary resources. Reading this text will equip elementary school educators with knowledge and skills to develop high-level thinking tasks and assessments.

The first chapter defines critical thinking and establishes the importance of infusing critical thinking skills into instruction. Teaching critical thinking skills prepares students for P–12 assessments, high-level college expectations, employers' demands, and challenging life situations. Training students to think critically enables them make logical judgments and decisions and solve problems.

In the second chapter the levels of the revised Bloom's cognitive taxonomy (Anderson & Krathwohl, 2001) are described in great detail. Vignettes at the beginning of each section showcase real-life examples of the thinking levels. In addition, numerous examples of instructional tasks and assessments at each level are identified.

The third chapter identifies prevailing misconceptions associated with the taxonomy and problems associated with designing high-level thinking tasks and assessments. Using interpretive exercises is presented as one solution to increase the level of critical thinking in instructional tasks and assessments.

In the fourth chapter, scenarios, real-world examples, and authentic tasks are described as a method to assess students in a close to real-world context, along with an explanation of how these can be used to boost higher-level thinking. Design tips are included along with numerous examples from a variety of subject areas.

Next, in Chapter 5, visuals are identified as a method to increase the thinking levels in assessment. Visuals include illustrations, maps, diagrams, data tables, and charts that appeal to visual learners while also engaging them in higher-level thinking. This chapter describes each of these types of pictorial representations and how they can be integrated into instructional tasks and assessments. As with the scenarios in the previous chapter, design tips are included along with numerous examples from a variety of subject areas.

In Chapter 6, short quotes, passages, and media clips are presented as another approach to challenge students to understand, analyze, and evaluate information. The text describes ways to utilize quotes, passages, and media clips in instruction and assessment while addressing how they can enhance higher-level thinking. Again, design tips are included along with numerous examples from a variety of subject areas.

Chapter 7 showcases ways to build a thinking culture in a classroom along with ideas to embed interpretive exercises into formative and summative assessments. The final chapter summarizes the text and challenges the reader to establish a plan with specific goals to implement the ideas presented in the text. By learning the knowledge and skills to develop high-level thinking tasks and assessments, elementary school educators will be more prepared to lead classrooms where students engage in meaningful learning experiences.

Importance of Critical Thinking

Too often we give children answers to remember rather than problems to solve.

—Roger Lewin

When I was a principal, one day the cafeteria manager reported that a student threw a strawberry during lunch. The student vehemently denied committing such an atrocious offense. Therefore, I conducted further interviews with students sitting at his table and near where the strawberry landed. All the stories pointed toward the accused student as the culprit. I asked the strawberry thrower to please clean up the table and floor where the strawberry was thrown. After several requests he adamantly refused to clean up the area, so I assigned him to the alternative learning area for the rest of the day. His guardian was informed of the incident. Several hours later I heard yelling in the front office, and the secretary informed me that the strawberry thrower's mother wanted to speak to me. I invited her back to my office to discuss the incident. I tried to explain how I had investigated the situation; however, she refused to sit down and proceeded to defend her child, insisting that he would never throw anything. My attempts to calm her down were futile. Holding her cell phone up in the air with fingers on the numbers, she finally shrieked, "I am going to call 911!" At that moment I just stood looking at her, not knowing how to proceed. Although I had enjoyed an excellent undergraduate and graduate education, I did not remember anything in my coursework suggesting how to handle an irate mom calling 911 over a strawberry tossed across the lunchroom. I suspect even Google couldn't have helped me here.

Life is complex. We all face similar situations when understanding complicated issues is critical to addressing the problem. The workplace and the world are rapidly evolving with abundant information and massive technological advances. How can we prepare our students to rapidly and successfully adapt to the changing world and complex circumstances they will encounter? We teach them to think! Thinking skills should be infused into daily instruction to adequately prepare students for college, careers, and life. Without these skills, students cannot effectively analyze multiple sources of information, draw logical conclusions, and create innovative solutions for problems.

What Is Critical Thinking?

It is easy to define what critical thinking is not—a memorized answer or reactive thinking. Critical thinking is not a simplistic recalling of previous information or illogical and irrational thinking. Reactive thinking is instinctive. For example, a buyer who desires a large-ticket item might immediately buy it without considering whether she has sufficient money, has space for the item, or needs the item.

People who disdain critical thinking often jump to conclusions, fail to recognize biases, and are unwilling to consider various perspectives. Weak critical thinkers address a problem or challenge by failing to understand and organize the important facts of the situation, being distracted by unimportant information, lacking perseverance to solve the problem, and designing a vague solution, not appropriate to the specific situation (Facione, 2011). Do you know people like this? All people have times in their lives when they might exhibit some characteristics of weak critical thinkers.

There are various definitions of critical thinking. According to Chaffee (1988), critical thinking is "our active, purposeful, and organized effort to make sense of our world by carefully examining our thinking, and the thinking of others, in order to clarify and improve our understanding" (p. 29). Critical thinking is analytical and deliberate and involves original thinking. Critical thinking is deeply processing knowledge to identify connections across disciplines and find potential creative solutions to problems. Critical thinkers use reflective decision-making and thoughtful problem-solving to analyze situations, evaluate arguments, and draw appropriate inferences. Critical thinkers have a passion to seek the truth even when the truth may contradict long-held beliefs.

The Partnership for 21st Century Skills (2011) has identified four areas of critical thinking skills: (1) reasoning effectively, (2) using systems thinking, (3) making judgments and decisions, and (4) solving problems. (See Figure 1.1.) These thought processes often require students to examine multiple information sources and identify key information relevant to the task. Critical thinkers often possess a probing inquisitiveness, zealous dedication to understanding, eagerness to obtain reliable information or evidence, and purposeful, reflective judgment based on consideration of evidence. To make informed decisions and evaluate the impact of actions, critical thinkers use multiple thought processes at once. To teach students how to appropriately approach multifaceted problems, questions, and decisions, schools must design curriculum that replicates the complicated nature of the real world.

Figure 1.1   **21st Century Critical Thinking Skills**

Reason Effectively
◆ Use various types of reasoning (inductive, deductive, etc.) as appropriate to the situation

Use Systems Thinking
◆ Analyze how parts of a whole interact with each other to produce overall outcomes in complex systems

Make Judgments and Decisions
◆ Effectively analyze and evaluate evidence, arguments, claims and beliefs ◆ Analyze and evaluate major alternative points of view ◆ Synthesize and make connections between information and arguments ◆ Interpret information and draw conclusions based on the best analysis ◆ Reflect critically on learning experiences and processes

Solve Problems
◆ Solve different kinds of non-familiar problems in both conventional and innovative ways ◆ Identify and ask significant questions that clarify various points of view and lead to better solutions

Source: From The Partnership for 21st Century Skills (2011). *21st century critical thinking skills.* Copyright 2013 Eye On Education, Inc. Reprinted with permission of The Partnership for 21st Century Skills.

With higher-level thinking tasks, classrooms can promote an intellectually stimulating learning environment that prepares students for the 21st century.

Importance of Critical Thinking

Global changes are directly impacting education. With increasingly complex jobs, global interdependence, and technological advances, the expectations for workforce skills are evolving. Workforce demands are leaving low-skilled workers with few options for other careers. Life choices are complex due to the proliferation of a variety of information that can be inaccurate and biased. Without refined critical thinking skills, erroneous information can negatively impact life decisions. In order to counteract these changes, students must be equipped with thinking skills to deliberately examine information and make logical decisions.

Several benefits arise from practicing and refining students' critical thinking skills. Embedding critical thinking skills in the curriculum helps sustain an educated citizenry; prepares students for college, future careers, and life situations; and primes students to meet mandates of state and national tests and standards.

Sustaining Democracy

Thinking skills are vital in sustaining a democratic government. When citizens utilize critical thinking, countries can make good judgments about the best course of action. With critical thinking skills, individual citizens can effectively examine various candidates for election, decide how to act if they disagree with government measures, and carefully review opposing evidence as a jury member and make a sound decision based on facts. Since education is the primary means for preparing students to be citizens, schools should focus on embedding these skills in instructional tasks and assessments. Schools have the job of inculcating these skills in all students in order to prevent democracies from being led by the elite. Maintaining a democracy requires that all citizens possess an ability to critically engage in democratic functions.

College, Career, and Life Success

The Partnership for 21st Century Skills (2011) advocates merging the 3Rs (core academic content mastery) and the 4Cs (critical thinking and problem-solving, collaboration, communication, and creativity and innovation). (See Figure 1.2.) Fusing these skills together can prepare students for success in college, career, and life. While students may forget the specific content of their classes, critical thinking is a skill that prepares them to adapt to changing circumstances in the 21st century.

Figure 1.2 **Partnership for 21st Century Skills: Framework for 21st Century Learning**

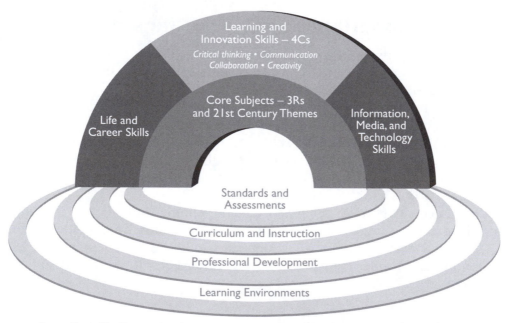

Source: From The Partnership for 21st Century Skills (2011). *Partnership for 21st century skills: Framework for 21st century learning.* Copyright 2013 Eye On Education, Inc. Reprinted with permission of The Partnership for 21st Century Skills.

College Success

High schools have been criticized for not adequately preparing students for the level of rigor they will encounter in college (Achieve, 2006). The ACT test, which is used as a measure of college and career readiness, defines if students will be able to be successful in first-year courses at a postsecondary institution without the assistance of remediation courses. ACT's College Readiness Benchmarks identify minimum scores needed on the ACT subject area tests to predict a 50 percent chance of obtaining a B or higher or a 75 percent chance of obtaining a C or higher in a first-year college course. In 2011, 66 percent of high school graduates taking the ACT met the English College Readiness Benchmark. Twenty-five percent successfully passed all four College Readiness Benchmarks. Twenty-eight percent of high school students did not pass any of the College Readiness Benchmarks. ACT reports that these test scores remained essentially the same between 2007 and 2011 (ACT, 2011). ACT predictions have been confirmed: nearly one-third of students entering some type of postsecondary education take remedial courses in one or more subjects because they lack the skills to take standard credit-bearing courses (National Center for Education Statistics, 2011).

ACT research shows a positive benefit of a rigorous core preparatory curriculum for all students. A rigorous curriculum would include foundational skills that adequately prepare students for college-level work. The *Ready to Succeed* report states, "Students enrolled in such a curriculum earn higher scores on the ACT, are better prepared to enter the workplace and/or credit-bearing college courses, show increased persistence in postsecondary education, and have significantly greater chances of earning college degrees and succeeding in the workplace" (ACT, 2006, p. 2).

Increasing the level of critical thinking skills in any program raises the level of rigor. Critical thinking has been cited as a key factor in student success in college. In a study of college seniors, students' level of critical thinking was predictive of their cumulative college grade point average (Torres, 1993). In a study to examine thinking skills, including problem-solving and creativity, Sternberg (2008) gave tests to college freshmen and high school seniors. The findings showed that this test predicted students' grades as college freshmen twice as well as SAT scores and high school grade point averages. Similarly, in a study of 1,100 college students, critical thinking tests significantly correlated with college grade point averages (Facione, 1990a, 1990b). In 2011, a research study surveyed teachers, parents, students, and Fortune 100 executives to determine what were the key areas to prepare students for college and career readiness. Two areas emerged with 90 percent agreement among all groups: problem-solving skills and critical thinking skills (MetLife, 2011). Therefore, embedding critical thinking experiences into the school curriculum can have a positive impact on students' potential for college success.

Career Success

Critical thinking skills are imperative in any job. For example, doctors are expected to listen carefully to a patient's account of medical ailments, review prior conditions, consider medical knowledge, and utilize prior experiences to treat the condition accurately and efficiently. Possessing critical thinking skills is required for professional positions. Employers expect that their employees use reasoned judgment. One superintendent I know commented that the number-one quality that he desired in a principal is common sense when approaching complex problems.

The Conference Board (2006) conducted a survey of human resource professionals and found that 70 percent of employees with a high school education were lacking in critical thinking skills. This statistic is worrying considering that routine jobs are increasingly being replaced by computerized machines. Basic skills hence are insufficient for job survival. Businesses want workers who utilize critical thinking skills for decision-making, independent thinking, and problem-solving (Silva, 2008). For example, hotel front-desk clerks used to provide check-in services; however, now some hotels provide online check-in. Front-desk clerks are evolving, as are employees in many other careers, into workers who use their critical thinking abilities to solve customers' problems. Businesses expect that even workers who move from high school directly into the workforce need to possess critical thinking skills to handle the myriad challenges they will encounter.

With the global economy, low-skill jobs are moving to other countries with cheaper labor forces. In order for the United States to maintain the high-skill positions, it must have an educational system that will prepare students for the new economy where rapid change demands that workers think and innovate. Workers are increasingly expected to collect information from various sources and to critically interpret information. The National Center on Education and the Economy (2008) states, "creativity and innovation are the keys to the good life, in which high levels of education—a very different kind of education than most of us have had—are going to be the only security there is" (p. 24). Employees are more valuable if they can solve problems and reason thoughtfully. To prepare students to meet employers' expectations, schools have a responsibility to provide multiple opportunities for students to enhance their thinking skills, deal with abstractions, and innovate.

Life Success

Have you heard a teenager talking about purchasing a car based on only the model and color without considering other important details like the quality of the engine? I am sure we all can remember instances in our lives when we failed to use sound thinking. I am embarrassed to say that I too failed to employ critical thinking skills appropriately when I selected a boyfriend in high school. My criteria were limited to one—essentially, did he have a car? Surely, you recall similar decisions that lacked good thinking.

Poor thinking can result in bad decisions affecting not just ourselves but people around us. Failing to utilize critical thinking skills causes many negative consequences: job loss, academic failure, financial problems, and family violence. Failing to consider financial decisions thoughtfully can lead to frivolous purchases and bankruptcy. Students settle for low-skill jobs that allow them to begin earning money quickly because they fail to understand the potentially higher earnings they can get with a specialized degree.

How many of our students are not prepared to make good choices in life because they have not learned to examine the details of the situation, clarify the problem, eliminate extraneous information, generate a list of good solutions, and select the best option? If all our students were good at this, there would be fewer disciplinary referrals. Life is about complex choices: selecting a career, choosing among housing options, and sometimes selecting a mate. In essence, critical thinking is essential for survival and self-sufficiency. It moves students from intellectual dependence to independence.

National Standards

The importance of critical thinking is noted in the new national standards. The Common Core State Standards (CCSS) initiative directly identifies higher-order thinking skills as critical to achieving career and college readiness for all students. To meet the demand for students to be college and career ready, the language arts standards identify the following behaviors of a 21st-century literate person:

> [Students] habitually perform the critical reading necessary to pick carefully through the staggering amount of information available today in print and digitally. ... They reflexively demonstrate the cogent reasoning and use of evidence that is essential to both private deliberation and responsible citizenship in a democratic republic. (National Governors Association Center for Best Practices, 2010a, p. 3)

This vision for the Common Core State Standards clearly shows the emphasis on deep-thinking tasks. Similarly, the first three Common Core State Standards of mathematical practice are to "Make sense of problems and persevere in solving them," "Reason abstractly and quantitatively," and "Construct viable arguments and critique the reasoning of others" (National Governors Association Center for Best Practices, 2010b, p. 6). All these mathematical standards embody cognitively demanding tasks. As educators pursue CCSS alignment, then, it is crucial to design curricula and assessment systems that emphasize authentic real-world problems, engage students in inquiry and exploration, and provide opportunities for students to apply what they know in meaningful ways.

Preparation for State and National Tests

High-stakes testing has intensified the accountability of teachers and schools. More and more national assessments are embedding critical thinking questions; for example, the SAT now includes an analytic essay. Punitive sanctions and negative reports to the public due to low student achievement have caused schools to examine curriculum and assessments carefully to ensure they are aligned to state and national standards both in the content and in the level of thinking required. Cognitively demanding tasks provide the means to equip students to learn well. Shepard (2001) advocates for standards-based reform with challenging curriculum for all students focused on higher-order thinking skills and deep conceptual understanding.

Critical thinking promotes academic growth. In fact, intentionally teaching thinking skills is associated with increased test scores (Wenglinsky, 2000, 2002, 2003). Learning targets, strategies, and assessments requiring higher levels of thinking have been found to positively impact student learning (Raths, 2002). Furthermore, research shows that SAT scores significantly correlate with scores on critical thinking instruments in numerous studies (Facione, Facione, & Giancarlo, 1992; Jacobs, 1995; Frisby, 1992), as do ACT scores (Mines, King, Hood, & Wood, 1990; King, Wood, & Mines, 1990). When critical thinking skills are integrated into instruction, students will possess a deeper-level understanding of concepts (Swartz & Parks, 1994). This deeper level of understanding helps students perform at a higher level on state and national tests. Though critical thinking tasks may take longer for students to complete due to the time required to process their thinking, schools focusing on reasoning and thinking skills will reap the benefits with higher test scores.

Student Motivation

Recently, a high school teacher who had previously attended one of my trainings contacted me, stating that her students were unmotivated. For several days in a row, her lessons included fill-in-the-blank worksheets where students recorded definitions. She said that the assignments were easy, but several students were refusing to complete them. After listening to her account, I suggested that perhaps students were not completing the assignments *because* they were simple. While some teachers make classroom activities easy in order to encourage students to complete the assignments, sometimes students see the assignment as not worth their time—mere busywork.

In *The Silent Epidemic* (Civic Enterprises, 2006), a report based upon responses from high school dropouts, 66 percent of the dropouts said they would have given more effort to their work if their teachers had had higher expectations. According to Blackburn (2008), the idea that "students do not like hard work" is a misconception; "actually, students associate feelings of success and satisfaction with challenging work" (pp. 30, 31). Students notice busywork and respond in turn with low motivation, but when an authentic problem requires thinking skills, they are more motivated to complete the task. When teachers design cognitively complex assignments requiring students to analyze relationships and evaluate the best plans involving real-world topics, the students engage in the content in a meaningful and invigorating way. These instructional tasks actively engage students in complex problems while constructing meaning, a process that can transform students into attentive, eager, high-level thinkers.

Summary

People with refined critical thinking skills are able to understand the world around them and make good decisions. These skills are absolutely critical for sustaining democratic governments, increasing levels of college preparedness, improving employability, making life decisions, performing on educational assessments, and increasing student motivation. Clearly, the benefits for integrating critical thinking into the curriculum are apparent. Our job as educators, then, is to create opportunities for students to develop and enhance these skills.

Understanding the importance of critical thinking is the first step. This text will examine various levels of thinking. Since there are many misconceptions about these levels, this book initially delves into the revised Bloom's cognitive taxonomy (Anderson & Krathwohl, 2001) to build understanding of each level and its cognitive processes. With a clear understanding of this framework, educators will be able to assess the level of thinking in their classrooms. The third chapter will identify prevailing misconceptions associated with the taxonomy and its implementation and provide a solution to increase the level of cognitive complexity in instructional tasks and assessments, using interpretive exercises. The successive three chapters demonstrate how to incorporate interpretive exercises using scenarios, visuals, and quotes. Finally, the seventh chapter shares ideas on how to establish a culture of thinking in a classroom along with techniques to embed interpretive exercises into formative and summative assessments. At the end of each chapter are discussion questions to spark thinking with colleagues in small groups, teams, or professional learning communities. Additionally, each chapter concludes with a *Take Action* section to assist teachers in making practical applications of the knowledge presented in each chapter. Resources, including rubrics, assessments, evaluation tools, and other materials, are included to support teachers in this work.

Discuss

◆ What do you think is the most compelling reason for students to be taught critical thinking?

◆ What is the most important reason to include critical thinking skills in your curriculum?

◆ What are the consequences of *not* teaching critical thinking?

◆ Describe an example when a lack of critical thinking had a negative impact on your life.

Take Action

Using the assessment in Figure 1.3, Characteristics of Strong Critical Thinkers, rate your own level of critical thinking and the average level of the students in your class.

◆ How can you personally become a better critical thinker?

◆ How can you raise the level of critical thinking in your classroom?

◆ Which critical thinking attributes could you promote in your classroom instruction?

◆ What activities would you use to integrate those attributes into your instruction?

Figure 1.3 **Characteristics of Strong Critical Thinkers**

Self Assessment	Class Assessment	*Rate yourself and the general level of class critical thinking skills. Assign a value from 1 to 10 to each critical thinking attribute, with higher numbers used to show which attributes best describe you.*
		Inquisitiveness with regard to a wide range of issues
		Concern to become and remain well-informed
		Alertness to opportunities to use critical thinking
		Self-confidence in one's own abilities to reason
		Open-mindedness regarding divergent world views
		Flexibility in considering alternatives and opinions
		Understanding of the opinions of other people
		Fair-mindedness in appraising reasoning
		Honesty in facing one's own biases, prejudices, stereotypes, or egocentric tendencies
		Prudence in suspending, making, or altering judgments
		Willingness to reconsider and revise views where honest reflection suggests that change is warranted

Source: Adapted from Insight Assessment. (n.d.). *Characteristics of strong critical thinkers.* Copyright 2013 Eye On Education, Inc. Reprinted with permission of Insight Assessment.

Applying Bloom's Taxonomy in Your Classroom

*Thinking leads man to knowledge. He may see and hear, and read and learn,
as much as he pleases; he will never know any of it, except that which he has
thought over, that which by thinking he has made the property of his mind.
Is it then saying too much if I say, that man by thinking only becomes truly
man? Take away thought from man's life, and what remains?*

—Johann Heinrich Pestalozzi

Critical thinking as applied to K–12 schools was foundationally established
in 1956 when Benjamin Bloom edited the text titled *Taxonomy of Educational
Objectives* (Bloom, 1956). This handbook established a taxonomy or classification system for cognitive objectives. Bloom's work was recognized by
teachers, administrators, and curriculum specialists as a way to examine the
degree of thinking in classrooms. The taxonomy included six levels: Knowledge, Comprehension, Application, Analysis, Synthesis, and Evaluation.

With new understandings about education, in 2001 the framework was
revised by a group who worked for five years to clarify the taxonomy (Anderson & Krathwohl, 2001). The dimensions on the taxonomy are similar, but
the highest two levels on the framework have been interchanged. Evaluation
is now the fifth level and Creation, previously termed Synthesis, is at the top
level of the taxonomy. In the 2001 framework, the dimensions also shifted
to verb form to indicate the cognitive skill expected at each level. The levels now are Remember, Understand, Apply, Analyze, Evaluate, and Create.
(See Figure 2.1.) The revised version identifies significantly more cognitive
processes under each level to clarify the level of thinking in each category.
The revised taxonomy includes nineteen cognitive processes classified in six
categories. Previously it was considered that basic levels of understanding
must be mastered before higher levels could be addressed. Now, on many
occasions students may begin even at the highest level of Create and learn
low-level knowledge while engaging in a high-level thinking assignment.

Figure 2.1 **Changes in Bloom's Taxonomy Cognitive Levels**

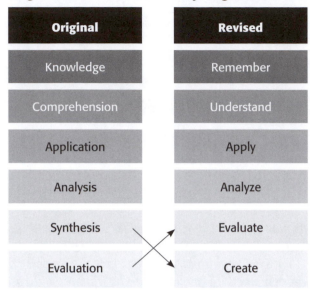

Retention versus Transfer

Educators have long discussed the importance of transferring new knowledge versus simply retaining information for the short term. Retention is the ability to recall information at a later time in a similar situation. Transfer is the ability to utilize previously learned information or skills in a new situation (Mayer & Wittrock, 1996). Retention involves recalling facts, like the definition of a tragedy. While facts can be memorized, recalling facts alone cannot solve unfamiliar or complex problems. Recalling facts is represented on the lowest levels of Bloom's taxonomy. Robert Reich (1989) characterized the education system as an assembly line, where students learn "long lists of facts that 'every adult should know' and standardized tests produce robots adept at Trivial Pursuit but unable to think for themselves or to innovate for the future" (p. 100).

Teaching to make sure students retain information is very different from teaching for transfer. Teaching students to make meaningful connections and transfer requires that students engage in cognitively demanding tasks at the higher levels of Bloom's taxonomy. The benefit of this level of learning is that it is preserved in the memory for longer periods of time; students can use information to determine answers to test questions, apply concepts to work situations, and even make good life decisions. If students evaluate how characters approach tragic life circumstances in literature, for example, it could help them guide a friend on how to handle difficult circumstances in real life. When students are able to transfer learning to new situations, meaningful learning occurs (Anderson & Krathwohl, 2001).

Revised Cognitive Levels for Bloom's Taxonomy

As explained previously, the revised Bloom's cognitive taxonomy includes six levels: Remember, Understand, Apply, Analyze, Evaluate, and Create. Subordinate cognitive processes are identified within each of the six levels to further describe the level of cognitive complexity. Bloom's cognitive levels and processes are summarized below. To clarify each cognitive process, vignettes of real-world instances and assessment examples are provided.

Level 1: Remember

Remembering, the first level of the taxonomy, involves retrieving information from the memory. At the Remember level the expectation is that the information is presented in some form and the student will retain it and be able to produce it later in a similar way as it was presented. A metaphor of the Remember level is a copy machine. Whatever the operator commands it to do, it does. The copy machine will not change the image unless directed to do so by the operator. The image is replicated exactly unless the operator instructs the machine to configure it another way. Students answer questions exceptionally well on this level because little thinking is required, only remembering.

Possessing factual knowledge is critical for higher levels of thinking. While memorizing the basic components of a sentence, a noun and a verb, is a Remember-level activity, without this knowledge writing would be an arduous task. Thus, Remember-level knowledge is a necessary foundation for more complex thought processes. In essence, a strong knowledge base allows students to effectively solve critical thinking problems (Sternberg, 2008). There are two cognitive processes in the Remember level: Recognizing and Recalling.

Remember-Level Cognitive Process: Recognizing

> *An American high school student visits Japan as an exchange student and comes to love a certain dish, tempura. Years later she tells her husband that this was her favorite dish. While visiting a Japanese restaurant, his wife exclaims "Oh, they have my favorite dish." Her husband immediately points to tempura on the menu.*

In this vignette, the husband sees tempura on the menu and recognizes it as his wife's favorite dish because of an earlier conversation. Students' ability to recognize information after it has been presented, as in this scenario, is a low-level task. In the Recognizing level, the learner searches for the memorized answer in the information provided. To assess students' ability to recognize, teachers can use forced-choice or selected-response assessments such as multiple-choice, true-false, matching, or fill-in-the-blank questions.

Another example: in a typing class, the teacher shows the students how to hold their hands on the keyboard. On the assessment, the teacher provides three pictures and the students must identify which one shows their hands in the correct typing position.

Classroom Example Remember Level: Recognizing
In-class instruction:
Students memorize the definition of an associative property.
Assessment:
When adding more than two numbers, the grouping of the addends does not change the sum. Which property is described in the previous statement? a. **associative property** b. distributive property c. commutative property

Remember-Level Cognitive Process: Recalling

> *While Joyce is eating at a restaurant, a former student comes to the table. "Hi, how are you? Do you remember me? You were my teacher in eighth grade."*
>
> *Joyce stares at her. Six years have passed since she had this student in class and the girl's face and hair have changed considerably. "Oh, you were in the group that did the Civil War play. Weren't you? Yes, your name is Hannah."*
>
> *"I can't believe you remember my name," Hannah says.*
>
> *Joyce thinks to herself, "Me too," because sometimes recalling former students' names is a difficult endeavor.*

Closely related to Recognizing, Recalling requires learners to remember relevant information to complete the task in an open-ended question or fill-in-the-blank assessment format. In this vignette, Joyce has to summon Hannah's name from her memory. Many teachers use this cognitive process when questioning. For example, a teacher states the definition of the term "evaporation." To check students' understanding, the teacher then asks students to recite the definition of the term. In this case, students are retrieving information from their memory. The game show *Jeopardy* represents thinking at this level. Many of the *Jeopardy* questions are difficult because they are obscure, but they do not require high levels of thinking because contestants are recalling information from memory.

In-class instruction:

Students memorize the definition of an associative property.

Assessment:

Directions: Fill in the blank below.

When adding more than two numbers, the grouping of the addends does not change the sum. Which property is described in the previous statement?

_____

 Level 2:
Understand

At the Remember level, information can quickly be recalled from the brain's short-term memory, but without deeper thinking, information can be discarded without moving to the long-term memory. Students often memorize information to pass a test and a day later cannot retrieve the information. Teaching primarily at the Remember level is like a spray of a water hose on a hot day. While you might get wet for a moment, in a few minutes the water evaporates. Life is not a Trivial Pursuit game in which recalling isolated facts will lead to success. To move beyond memorization and acquiring knowledge, the Understand level involves logical thinking. Knowing is different from understanding.

The Understand level is the beginning of original thinking. Students are not retrieving information memorized; they are building new connections in their minds. Just as a lightbulb connects to the power source and produces light, at the Understand level students develop new understandings. Paul and Elder (2005) state, "There is no way to impact, transfer, or inject the system in the mind of another person in pre-fabricated form. It cannot be put on a mental compact disk and downloaded into the mind without an intellectual struggle" (p. 13). At the Understand level, students receive information in oral, written, or graphic form and make meaning of the information. Cognitive development is an active process whereby students construct meaning in their minds. As Paul and Elder further comment, "To begin to take ownership one needs to give voice to those basic concepts;—e.g., to state what the concept means in one's own words; to elaborate what the concept means, again in one's own words; and then to give examples of the concept from real-life situations" (p. 10). These ideas are represented at the Understand level.

At the Understand level and the other four higher levels of the taxonomy, examples or tasks must be novel to provide a new challenge for students. If the teacher asks students to summarize a passage and the student is later asked to produce the same summary again, the second time it is presented it will be at the Remember level, recalling previously stored information. Instead, the teacher should select new examples or novel tasks in order to present different stimuli to challenge student thinking and reach the Understand and higher levels of Bloom's taxonomy.

The Understand level of thinking has seven cognitive processes, far more than the other levels. A tremendous amount of teaching and learning in schools is on this level as students build conceptual knowledge. During oral questioning, teachers ask students to summarize what others have stated, relate topics to their previous knowledge, provide additional examples of a concept or idea, and make connections between various concepts. All these ideas are encapsulated at the Understand level. The Understand level cognitive processes are Interpreting, Exemplifying, Classifying, Summarizing, Inferring, Comparing, and Explaining.

Understand-Level Cognitive Process: Interpreting

David enjoys smartphone technology and uses it to take lots of pictures of his family. At a meeting, Stacy starts viewing David's pictures.

"So Jordan played softball this year."

In the pictures there was no text. So how did Stacy draw that conclusion? David's daughter, Jordan, was wearing black shorts, a pink T-shirt emblazoned with the word "Sparklers," and a cap. Posed with her hand on her hip, she was smiling while holding a baseball bat. Stacy interpreted the picture by converting the visual image into words.

Interpreting involves changing information from one form to another. Students can convert text into pictures, graphics, music, and paraphrases. After reading a passage or listening to a speaker, students can create pictures that summarize the text (text to pictures). Students could also create a diagram to show the sequence of events in the story (text to graphics). After viewing a picture or graphic, students could explain what it means (picture or graphic to text). After reading a passage, students could paraphrase what was said in their own words (words to paraphrasing). Students could also put their information in musical form by imaginatively changing the lyrics of a song to represent the summary of the plot in a story or the summary of a historic culture (words to music). Another creative way is to have students use their body position or hand motions to represent a concept. For instance, students could create hand motions that represent vocabulary words.

Classroom Example
Understand Level: Interpreting

In-class instruction:

Students read in their textbook about the concept of democracy and paraphrase what the authors say about the term.

Assessment:

Create a picture that represents your conceptual understanding of democracy.

Understand-Level Cognitive Process: Exemplifying

> *At a faculty meeting, Ty says to his teaching partner, Julie, "Michael is really demure."*
>
> *"Oh, there you go using those big words again," Julie comments. "What does that mean?"*
>
> *"Well, he acts like Chad around others," Ty responds.*
>
> *"Oh, so you're saying he's modest and reserved. It might be because he's a new teacher. When I was a new teacher, I was demure too."*

Another cognitive process within the Understand level is Exemplifying. Students are often asked to provide another example of a concept; that is Exemplifying. In the vignette, the word "demure" is connected to another faculty member who acts in a similar fashion. By giving an example, Ty clarifies the meaning of the term. The following are some Exemplifying activities:

◆ **Social studies:** After discussing ancient Greek democracy, students provide a situation in their life where they see similar democratic principles at work.

◆ **Language arts:** While reading a book, students examine the concept of theme in the text. To assess their understanding of theme, students describe a fairy tale that has a similar theme or, in a multiple-choice format, select the title of another text they have already read that has a similar theme.

◆ **Science:** After studying examples of water conservation, students describe another way they can conserve water at home.

In their examples, students might be asked to provide another instance of the concept from within the discipline, another discipline, or their life. Challenging students to make connections across disciplines and to their life or prior knowledge builds greater meaning for students.

Classroom Example
Understand Level: Exemplifying

In-class instruction:

Students read about compounds and list H_2O as an example of a compound.

Assessment:

Which of the following is a compound?

    a. potassium (K)

    b. salt (NaCl)

    c. iron (Fe)

    d. copper (Cu)

In this case, none of the choices above were listed in the text or discussed prior to the assessment.

Understand-Level Cognitive Process: Classifying

You receive an email that appears to be from the district office. The email discusses the district email system and then states that your email account is over capacity and that, in order to continue to use the system, you will need to provide the sender with your last name and password. This last part seems suspicious so you forward the email to your administrator because it seems to be a scam.

Classifying involves categorizing information or items based on similar characteristics. In the vignette above, the teacher recognizes attributes of a scam email message, particularly the request for the teacher's password, and thus classifies the message as a scam. Instead of taking a general concept and thinking of an example, as in Exemplifying, Classifying requires students to identify the key traits first and then determine the concept. Students engage in active cognitive processing by attending to stimuli and organizing information into meaningful chunks (Mayer, 1999). Chunking or grouping helps learners understand how items are alike and different.

The teacher can establish the categories and have students group information into those identified headings. For example, after listening to various musical pieces, students group the pieces by style. Additionally, a teacher might show a new instrument from another country and have students explain which musical family this instrument would fit into. In social studies, the students could read primary sources about early colonists and their environment and determine which region they lived in based on clues from the texts.

Classroom Example
Understand Level: Classifying

In-class instruction:

Students read about the differences between chemical and physical changes. Two examples of chemical and physical changes are provided in the text.

Assessment:

Students group examples in categories based on whether they involve chemical or physical changes.

Understand-Level Cognitive Process: Summarizing

Ms. Kim says to the class, "For tonight's homework, please read the chapter, noting the key vocabulary, and complete the assigned questions."

Juan, who was texting under his desk and didn't hear the instructions, taps Tarin sitting in front of him and asks, "What's the homework?"

Annoyed that she is repeating the directions, Tarin quickly says, "Read the chapter and do the questions."

Summarizing requires students to create a statement to represent a body of information. When we are asked to repeat information, we often simplify the message and summarize for the purpose of efficiency, as shown in the vignette. Teachers often use this strategy to assess students' understanding of the key points in the lesson. Teachers ask students to summarize by writing a three-word summary, compose a text message of less than thirty characters, develop a headline for a news article about the lesson, or read a journal article and write a title for it. Students could read, watch a video clip, or observe a natural event and summarize what happened. Students could also select, in a multiple-choice format, which statement best summarizes an information source. Students can use web technologies including Animoto, Glogster EDU, or Photo Peach to create short presentations integrating pictures and text to summarize information. To encourage artistic abilities, teachers can ask students to draw or paint a picture to summarize text.

In-class instruction:

Students read about the elements of art.

Assessment:

Write a paragraph that summarizes the ideas presented in the text about the elements of art.

Understand-Level Cognitive Process: Inferring

José never seems to complete homework. Mr. Frank wonders what could be the cause of this behavior: family challenges, lack of interesting assignments, or maybe assignments that are too easy or too hard. When the math class begins studying ellipses and parabolas, Mr. Frank assigns a real-life math problem to find the trajectory of a space launch based on the given information. Unexpectedly, José completes his homework and wants to discuss the assignment. To reinforce the learning, Mr. Frank provides another assignment requiring students to find the trajectory of a meteorite that could potentially crash to Earth. The next day in class, José again has his assignment completed and poses questions about other connections to space topics. Though Mr. Frank knows there are obviously many reasons for José's behavior, he concludes there seems to be a connection between his motivation to complete homework assignments and space topics.

Inferring is looking for a pattern or relationship between examples. Inferences can involve the use of inductive and deductive reasoning. Inductive reasoning establishes a sensible generalization from information supplied or reasons from the specific to a broader lens. For example, after a first day in your class, a student might conclude you are a dynamite teacher based on the introductory activity, your inviting classroom, and comments from previous students about your class. In contrast, deductive reasoning moves from general reasoning to the specific, as shown in the vignette. Mr. Frank starts with several potential reasons for the student's low motivation and eventually rules out several ideas after observing José's behavior.

People make inferences all the time. The process is so automatic that most of the time the brain immediately takes observations and begins putting the pieces together to draw conclusions. When inferences are based on limited proof, inaccurate conclusions can be drawn—for example, first impressions of people, based on their style of dress, body language, and speech, which due to inadequate evidence may or may not be accurate.

In a classroom, students could examine the motives for a person's actions. Students would list possible causes and then select the best reasons for the person's action. It is important that inferences be clear, logical, justifiable, and reasonable. Factual information is used to form a reasonable conclusion, but inferring means going beyond this information to understand knowledge in another area. Students utilize information from data, statements, evidence, situations, hypotheses, judgments, and other sources to draw reasonable inferences and conclusions.

Before learning about the proper usage of quotation marks, students could be given several sentences with quotation marks used in various ways. Students would then record the rules they infer for how to use quotation marks appropriately. Another way to provide opportunities for students to practice inferring is through analogy tasks. Analogy tasks require students to infer the relationship between objects, terms, or ideas. Students can examine the significant ways they are similar and make a conclusion about their connection.

Classroom Example
Understand Level: Inferring

In-class instruction:

Students examine input and output charts, identifying the rule.

Assessment:

Examine the input and output chart. Identify the rule.

a. **multiply by 6**

b. add by 10

c. subtract by 10

d. divide by 6

Input	Output
2	12
8	48
11	66
Rule:	

Understand-Level Cognitive Process: Comparing

It is time to renew your contract and select a new cell phone. To make a good decision, you search online to examine the features, prices, and available data plans of your two favorite phones.

Comparing involves examining two different items, situations, or ideas in order to identify the similarities or differences. Students might compare a literary figure to a present-day character in a film based on certain identified characteristics. Anderson and Krathwohl (2001) state, "Comparing includes finding one-to-one correspondences between elements and patterns in one object, event, or idea and those in another object, event, or idea" (p. 75). This strategy has been shown to have a powerful effect on learning (Marzano, Pickering, & Pollock, 2001).

Graphic organizers help students develop their comparisons by creating a chart with each comparison item as a column heading and the various categories for comparison as rows along the side of the chart. For example, students could compare soccer and basketball based on the rules, plays, penalties, and other areas. Or, students could create connection journals in which they compare events in history to their lives, the world, or other texts. When students make connections to their lives, their level of interest in the task increases (Vosniadou, 2001).

Metaphors and analogies can be a way to show comparisons. Metaphors can show connections between two items that are typically not related. Using a topic studied, the teacher can give students the metaphor or students can write their own metaphor making connections between objects, persons, events, or ideas. Students can explain the key characteristics that make the one-to-one connections between the two items. Student comparisons might include a personal connection. For example, students could explain how photosynthesis is like cars using gasoline. Creating metaphors or analogies encourages imaginative thinking.

Classroom Example
Understand Level: Comparing

In-class instruction:

Students discusses various American holidays.

Assessment:

We have studied many American holidays: Lincoln's Birthday, Washington's Birthday, Independence Day, Dr. Martin Luther King Jr. Day, Labor Day, Columbus Day, Veterans Day, Thanksgiving Day, Election Day, Flag Day, and Memorial Day.

   A. Select two of the holidays mentioned above.

   B. Explain three ways the two holidays are similar.

   C. Describe two ways the holidays are different.

Understand-Level Cognitive Process: Explaining

> *"John, why did you knock her books out of her hand?" the principal asks. There is a long silence.*
>
> *With head bowed, John says, "Because I like her."*
>
> *"I see, but, John, didn't you notice when you do that she gets really angry with you?" the principal comments. "I think there might be other ways to get her attention that would help her like you more. Would you like to discuss some alternative options?"*

Understanding means comprehending the basic cause-and-effect relationships. In this vignette, which occurs in schools many times, students attempt to flirt with other students and do not realize their attempts actually cause an opposite reaction from what they hoped. Explaining occurs when students make cause-and-effect connections between various ideas and concepts. It involves "constructing a cause-and-effect model, including each major part in a system or each major event in the chain, and using the model to determine how a change in one part of the system or one 'link' in the chain affects a change in another part" (Anderson & Krathwohl, 2001, p. 76). Sequencing or causal chains are taught with many concepts, such as the water cycle. Understanding the cyclical nature of certain systems helps to predict a reaction if one part of the cycle is interrupted. In English, characters in books display negative patterns of action that help readers predict the character's next action. By understanding the causal chain of events, students are able to comprehend the reason something happened and predict what might happen if similar instances occur. When working with cause-and-effect relationships, it is important to identify all contributory causes since in some instances there is more than one cause or multiple effects. If only one cause is considered, then the predicted effect might not be accurate.

Anderson and Krathwohl (2001) identify three areas for Explaining: troubleshooting, redesigning, and predicting. When troubleshooting, students encounter a problem and detect the cause of the problem. When redesigning, students examine the system and make changes to an identified purpose. When predicting, students think about how a change might impact other variables. Here are some examples of instructional tasks or assessment in these areas:

◆ **Troubleshooting:** A new invasive plant, kudzu, has been found in our community growing along the sides of several roads. Describe what possible ways this plant may have arrived in our community.

◆ **Redesigning:** Fewer students are eating healthy snacks at school. How can the school encourage healthy snacks?

◆ **Predicting:** Describe the effects if the South had won the Civil War or if voter turnout at the polls continues to decline.

Classroom Example
Understand Level: Explaining

In-class instruction:

Students identify the key characteristics needed for an organism to survive in a particular ecosystem.

Assessment:

When given the description of a fictitious animal, students explain whether the animal will survive in a given ecosystem.

 Level 3:
Apply

The third level of the revised cognitive taxonomy is Apply. In this level, there are certain procedures or steps that are expected to be followed to answer new problems. Thus, the teacher would model the appropriate steps to follow for a given example and then students would follow a similar procedure to answer a different problem. There are two cognitive processes in the Apply level: Executing and Implementing. The Apply level is primarily connected to procedural knowledge because of the expected order or procedure to be followed, particularly in the Executing cognitive process; however, conceptual knowledge can be involved in the Implementing cognitive process.

Apply-Level Cognitive Process: Executing

> *Shopping—people either seem to like it or hate it. Jan loves to get a good deal and often browses the items on the discounted racks. She finds an item she would like to buy on a rack under a sign that states everything is 50 percent off. The item costs $20, so she computes half of its price would be $10.*

In Executing, the student encounters a new example, but fairly quickly is able to see what procedure is needed. As in the scenario above, many people quickly calculate cost based on the percentage off. Computing this calculation is a routine skill using procedural knowledge taught in math classes. This cognitive process is well addressed in traditional math classes. The teacher models the procedure and then students complete additional problems repeating this method. For example, the teacher models how to solve problems using the quadratic formula. Students then apply the formula to different numbers and solve the equation. In science, the teacher models how to balance equations. Then students are asked to balance a new equation using the sequence the teacher just modeled. In an English class, students are taught how to appropriately use question marks. Students then receive a set of sentences and must correctly place the question mark at the end of each sentence. In social studies, students are taught how to find a specific location using longitude and latitude. Students then are given new points on a map and are expected to record the degrees of longitude and latitude for each location.

In-class instruction:

Students are taught about commas and semicolons and how to use them appropriately in sentences.

Assessment:

Correct the sentence below with the correct punctuation.

1. I want to go with you mom said I could.

Apply-Level Cognitive Process: Implementing

At Moss Middle School, there is an exciting new teaching position posted that you are interested in pursuing. The principal is a casual acquaintance. To pursue the position, it is recommended that you contact the principal. In high school, business letters and cover letters for résumés were clearly discussed. You write a letter, taking care to use a professional tone and format yet avoid being too formal and off-putting.

The Implementing cognitive process involves a murkier task than the Executing level. As in the example above, the casual acquaintance makes the task more challenging. Language that might be recommended in other business letters would not be appropriate for this situation due to the personal connection. At the Implementing level, the procedure that should be applied is not readily apparent and the student must think through which procedure to select. The problem could be complex, with several possible answers. Often procedural and conceptual knowledge is required to complete the task. At the highest level of Implementing, the learner could use conceptual knowledge to establish a procedure for a task (Anderson and Krathwohl, 2001).

Here are some examples of Implementing tasks:

◆ **Math:** Students are presented with three options for a hypothetical summer vacation. Each option has discounts with special promotions. Students are to determine which trip is the best deal.

◆ **Music:** Students will write two measures of music that use different types of notes (e.g., whole, half, quarter, eighth) and include tempo and dynamics markings in order to elicit a happy feeling when played.

Level 4:
Analyze

Analyze is the fourth level of the taxonomy. Just as a microscope takes a close view of each of the individual parts, the Analyze level involves breaking apart information to examine each section. The Analyze level requires students to utilize lower-level thinking skills, including the understandings, to identify the key elements first and then examine each part. Paul and Elder (2005) comment that high-performing students have the ability to accurately analyze problems and questions:

> [Students] gather information (distinguishing the relevant from the irrelevant), recognize key assumptions, clarify key concepts, use language accurately, identify (when appropriate) relevant competing points of view, notice important implications and consequences, and reason carefully from clearly stated premises to logical conclusions. (p. 15)

This describes many of the attributes of the Analyze level. The Analyze level is the foundation of higher-level skills on the Evaluate and Create levels (Anderson and Krathwohl, 2001). Often when the phrase "critical thinking" is used, it refers to the top three levels of Bloom's taxonomy: Analyze, Evaluate, and Create. A key component of critical thinking is the process of analyzing and assessing thinking with a view to improving it. Hence, many consider the Analyze level as the beginning of deep thinking processes. There are three cognitive processes in Analyze: Differentiating, Organizing, and Attributing. These three cognitive processes help students overcome some of the noted difficulties of thinking, including (a) impulsive conclusions, (b) failure to examine other points of view or identify assumptions, (c) unfocused or inexact thought processes, and (d) disorganized thinking (Perkins, 1995).

Analyze-Level Cognitive Process: Differentiating

"Mr. Harold, Mr. Harold!" said Summer. "I don't have my home-work done today. Last night I had a softball game. The field was far from my house. Did you hear about my hit? Oh, and our trip home was really long. My mom did not know the roads very well. I worked on my homework on the way home, but my brother kept yelling and the road was bumpy. Have you ever been on that road to that field? It has some really bad twists and turns and major potholes ..."

Have you ever had a student approach you with a story like this? As teachers we are constantly engaging in the cognitive process of Differentiating, judiciously examining content for relevant and irrelevant characteristics. In the above example, many of the pieces of information mentioned by the student are not important to address the problem of the student not having her homework.

Do students know how to identify which information is important and relevant to a situation? A teacher told me she wanted to test her students' ability to discern which numbers in a math problem were relevant to create an equation. In her real-world math problem she included some irrelevant numbers. For example, "I'm going to put a fence around my square yard. I measured one side and it is 150 yards. I left my phone number (745-4438) with the fencing specialist. He called me back 30 minutes later and asked me about the type of fencing I would like. Based on the information provided, how much fencing do I need?" Would you be surprised to find out many students tried to use both the 30 (minutes) and the phone number in their calculations? Clearly, they were not able to identify relevant information. But when people make real-world decisions, don't they often consider both relevant and irrelevant information? Often students jump to conclusions without really examining pertinent evidence, as in the fencing problem. Paul and Elder (2005) state, "Thinking can only be as sound as the information upon which it is based" (p. 23). Therefore, students need to know which information is important for a given situation.

Discriminating information is critical to survival in the real world. Sales-persons try to convince consumers to purchase items by including in their sales pitch irrelevant details that can distract consumers. To be information-ally literate, students must possess this skill to know which information to consider and which to reject.

To practice discriminating between relevant and irrelevant information, students can read texts or listen to information sources that present irrelevant details. When students find extraneous information, they can mark it out or highlight key sections.

◆ **Social studies:** Students can listen to political speeches and identify the point of the speech and the related and unconnected details or examples that are used to support the main ideas.

◆ **Language arts:** When writing a research paper, students could create a list of sources that provide support for their main idea. In order to complete this task, students must be able to read each source and identify if it provides relevant information to support the main idea. Many sources may be discarded before the final list of sources is determined.

Classroom Example
Analyze Level: Differentiating Example

In-class instruction:

Students read science informational texts to identify key ideas and pinpoint sentences that did not support the main idea.

Assessment:

After reading *The Magic School Bus Lost in the Solar System*, identify several sentences that support the main idea of the book. Locate five sentences that could be eliminated from the story because they do not focus on the main idea.

Analyze-Level Cognitive Process: Organizing

"Stop it," says nine-year-old Parker. "Ainsley's coming into my room and won't go away," he yells.

Hearing the commotion, the children's mother enters the room and asks what has happened. After hearing both sides explain what happened between Parker and his younger sister Ainsley, the mother is able to analyze the sequence of events to determine what really happened. She determines that Parker and Ainsley were kicking a ball. The ball hit Ainsley in the face, which caused her to get upset. To try to prevent her from getting more angry and telling on him, Parker started acting silly and tickling her. After she was in a better mood, Parker walked away to his room to play by himself. Ainsley, wanting to continue playing, repeatedly ran into Parker's room yelling childish phrases and quickly exiting, which annoyed him.

In the scenario above, the mother, through hearing both descriptions of the event, is able to sequence the events in order to examine the situation. With Organizing, students can create charts, diagram, flowcharts, other graphic organizers, or outlines to show connections among various pieces of information. With this cognitive process, students could construct charts to organize the key pieces of information, with varying designs from each student. Students could design organizers to show the multiple interactions occurring in a historical event, scientific results, and events in a reading. In a multiple-choice format, students could identify which organizer corresponds with the information source. An instructional strategy to practice this cognitive process is an inductive learning strategy: given a list of concepts, students group like concepts together by categorizing them and labeling what the concepts in the group have in common. With Organizing, students are grouping information together in a sensible way.

Math: Students review math problems worked incorrectly and create a diagram to depict how the student who did the math is off track.

Social studies: Students create an outline to depict the ideas present in the historical reading.

Classroom Example
Analyze Level: Organizing

In-class instruction:

Students scrutinize the plot structure of a story.

Assessment:

After reading a new story, students create a diagram to depict the key conflicts and their impact on plot development.

Analyze-Level Cognitive Process: Attributing

"Welcome to Fisher's! We have lots of cars to choose from here. What type of car would you like? Let me tell you about this car. It is very popular and affordable. We have payment plans . . . . Let's talk about your trade-in car. You'd be lucky to get a dollar for your car right now. But we'll give you $1,000. That's the book value. You can't believe the book values you see on Internet sites. Now let me tell you—this is a good deal. We're losing money on this deal!"

The world is filled with people trying to convince us to do or believe something. In our world, recognizing biases, assumptions, intentions, or points of view helps us critically examine information. It requires students to read between the lines—a step up from Inferring, an Understanding-level cognitive process. Often students examine information on the Internet without realizing that information posted online is not all credible. Many jobs require employees to examine information from various sources and identify the various biases and intentions.

With this cognitive process, students read or observe something and examine it to see if the information source has an underlying motive or bias. Many interest groups use persuasive messages to call for action. Students must be able to analyze various arguments and opinions while recognizing the perspectives presented. Students can discuss how various points of view can develop due to age, culture, social roles, employment, peer groups, religions, and gender.

Being open-minded to other viewpoints is often considered a trait of critical thinkers. Being open-minded means people are willing to consider divergent views and are aware of their own biases. An open-minded person respects the diverse opinions of others (Facione, 2011). Seeking information from divergent points of view and equally considering all viewpoints can help students with instructional tasks as well as conflict resolution, as parties are able to view information from various perspectives (Swartz & Parks, 1994). People have a natural tendency to favor their own position and interests while ignoring opposing arguments. With Attributing instructional tasks, students should be challenged to acknowledge their own assumptions and viewpoints that might involve prejudice, stereotypes, biases, and distortions. Assumptions are often (a) hidden or understated, (b) taken for granted, (c) influential in determining the conclusion, and (d) potentially deceptive (Browne & Keeley, 2004). By considering the assumptions of a writer or personal assumptions, students are able to analyze their own and others' thinking. Ultimately, the hope is to be able to judge objectively even if the conclusion is against their own self-interest.

For in-class experiences, students might analyze the various perspectives about a topic, considering opposing arguments and the reasons supporting each position. Any time various point of views are considered, classes can engage in healthy debate.

- ◆ **Social studies:** Students can examine historical writings to detect biases and points of view.

- ◆ **Language arts:** In *Charlotte's Web*, there are two clearly different points of view—the farmer's and the pig's. Students can pinpoint the perspectives and biases in the text.

- ◆ **Math and science:** Students can examine reports to determine the purpose for the data collection.

Classroom Example Analyze Level: Attributing
In-class instruction:
Students investigate various forms of alternative energy sources.
Assessment:
After reading articles on solar energy by a variety of authors, describe the differing viewpoints.

 # Level 5:
Evaluate

Evaluate is the fifth level of the taxonomy; typically the Analyze level and other lower cognitive processes are employed to engage in the Evaluate cognitive processes. In a courtroom, the judge makes a decision by weighing the evidence and deciding the best outcome or resources. At the Evaluate level, informational sources are examined to assess their quality and decisions are made based on the identified criteria. There are two cognitive processes in the Evaluate level: Checking and Critiquing.

Evaluate-Level Cognitive Process: Checking

> *The evidence is presented on both sides. One witness testifies for her mother and persuasively argues that her ex-husband hit her mother, causing major health problems. Health experts explain that the medical condition is due to blunt force trauma. The ex-husband clarifies that the mother refused to leave his house and, after an argument, he hit the mother. Now, it is the jury's responsibility to examine the facts.*

Juries are expected to scrutinize information in order to determine if the witnesses are credible and if the testimony is accurate. Anderson and Krathwohl (2001) state, "Checking involves testing for internal inconsistencies or fallacies in an operation or product" (p. 83). A fallacy or internal inconsistency is an error in reasoning where the ideas in an argument do not adequately support the conclusion. Open-mindedness and considering alternative systems of thought are important, but students also need a critical eye when considering alternative views. Students possessing this cognitive ability pursue unsubstantiated claims, question ideas, and demand validation for arguments, interpretations, assumptions, beliefs, or theories.

When evaluating an argument, first the reader should determine the issue and/or conclusion. The conclusions and the reasons should support the argument. Evidence provides the proof, and the reasons explain why (Browne & Keeley, 2004). One way to help students to evaluate is to teach them to make sure viewpoints are supported with appropriate reasons and evidence. To introduce this skill, students can examine the arguments in a commercial, identifying the claim and deciding whether each claim is supported by reasons and evidence. Shel Silverstein's poem titled "Smart" is a good way to introduce incorrect assumptions. The boy in the poem trades his one dollar and collects more coins with each trade, but actually ends up with less money, five pennies. However, the child feels he has more money now because he has more coins, even though the value of the coins is clearly less than the original amount.

Many students jump to conclusions or accept information without questioning the quality of the information. Students should practice evaluating information and sources. There are spoof websites that look deceptively real but have false information (Bradley, 2012). Using these sites in classroom instruction can teach students to carefully evaluate websites before using their information.

Many times on the news there are reports of new data. Are appropriate conclusions derived from the data? The common claim by students, "The teacher just doesn't like me," or by teachers, "Students just don't want to learn," can be a topic of conversation to engage students in this cognitive process. Students can examine the sources for credibility by assessing the reasonableness of ideas. Paul and Elder (2005) state that information should be examined based on its "clarity, accuracy, precision, relevance, depth, breadth, logic, and significance" (p. 12). There are many considerations when examining sources, including the following:

◆ **Author qualifications:** A work by an author should be considered a credible source if that author has a level of expertise in the area. However, even with that expertise, the source may have biases or special interests that distort the message. Additionally, evaluators should determine if the source is a primary or secondary account to assess the level of confidence that should be placed in the source.

◆ **Evidence:** A source should be supported by evidence. The reader should consider whether the evidence can be interpreted differently. The evidence should be accurate so as not to distort facts. Sometimes data are used inaccurately; thus the conclusions are inaccurate. When a conclusion or argument is posed, students should examine if the reasons provided support the idea. For example, in the magazine *Consumer Reports*, data are shown to support the recommendations.

◆ **Reliability of sources:** Evaluating the reliability of sources means considering whether other authorities agree. Even with a qualified author, more than one expert opinion can validate and corroborate information. Evaluators should determine if the source leaves out key information. The author may purposely include certain sources to support the message. For example, mass media and economic interests can spin messages to address their specific perspective. Also, with the rapidly changing information available, the date of publication can impact the reliability of the source (Chaffee, 2006).

To assess this cognitive process, students could conduct research on any topic and examine the print and media sources to evaluate whether the sources are credible and whether the conclusions are appropriately drawn from the informational source. Students might be able to draw other conclusions beyond what is mentioned. Most of these types of activities lead to essay or short-answer assessments.

- ◆ **English and social studies:** Students identify which source is the most reliable for a paper on political parties.

- ◆ **Science:** Students examine if the sources used in a science article posted online are appropriate and reliable.

Classroom Example
Evaluate Level: Checking

In-class instruction:

Students read about the physical effects of exercise on humans.

Assessment:

Read the article about a famous athlete. Identify one piece of information in the article that fails to support the author's case that hard work was the main reason for the athlete's exceptional athletic skills.

Evaluate-Level Cognitive Process: Critiquing

It's teacher evaluation time! You know the process. You will carefully prepare your lesson knowing an administrator will be evaluating you based on the state teacher standards. At the conclusion of the evaluation form, your strengths and areas for improvement are summarized.

Oh, a stressful time for teachers! Teacher evaluations are a good example of the Critiquing cognitive process. Critiquing involves assessing the value of an idea or product based on a set of criteria. The skill of decision-making is used in schools and in daily life to examine and then select from various choices (Sternberg, 2008). In schools, students seem to critique superficially almost every day as they state who is the best teacher (e.g., one that assigns no homework) or what car is the best to buy (e.g., of course, the one that is bright red). Without practice, students often rank choices based completely on personal preferences instead of developing logical criteria, thus making poor conclusions and decisions. Failing to build Critiquing skills leaves students unable to grapple with the complexities of life or to reasonably select the best option.

It seems the key decisions in life involve Critiquing, whether it is whom to marry, which house to purchase, or which career path to follow. Teaching students how to thoughtfully make reasoned decisions based on weighing the evidence prepares them for real-life situations they encounter. By learning how to evaluate, students can engage in healthy debates arguing a position, which many students enjoy doing.

To reach this level, first the decision or problem must be defined along with the explicit criteria to evaluate the options. The decision could relate to a professional, personal, or civic problem. It could ask the students the "best" way to do something. What is the best way to solve a multistep real-world problem? Which is the best candidate for the position? The criteria might need to be researched to ensure proper consideration of key areas. Criteria can be based on the effectiveness of the solution, safety, cost-effectiveness, and other factors. Next, options or choices that align to the decisions should be identified. Students must be open-minded and willing to consider other ideas, options, and information in order to develop alternatives (Klaczynski, 2001). It is important to have a classroom climate that is supportive of divergent opinions and solutions so all options are considered. If the options are novel ideas, students could be working at the Create level using the Generating cognitive process, which will be introduced in the next section. Next, students would explain with reasons how each option meets the criteria. Students might also rank the options or put the ideas on a continuum based on each idea meeting the criteria. Some criteria may be more important than others and thus be given more significant contemplation in ranking the alternatives. Some options might have important long- and short-term consequences to consider. If the options are not evaluated carefully with all pertinent information considered, decisions can be haphazard (Swartz & Parks, 1994). Finally, using convergent thinking, the best solution, idea, or product for a situation is selected.

Decision-Making Steps
1. Identify the problem or situation.
2. Secure relevant information.
3. Define criteria for evaluation.
4. Explore options.
5. Prioritize alternatives.

In schools, Critiquing exercises can be embedded in many areas. To prevent disciplinary infractions, school administrators often implore students to utilize this cognitive process to examine a course of action and whether it is effective. If Javon pushes Mark, what are now the long-term consequences? What other options does a student have to deal with the conflict? Here are some other examples:

◆ **Math:** Students select which family trip would be the best for their family based on established criteria and then develop a budget.

◆ **Language arts and social studies:** When studying historical figures or characters in a novel, students could identify who would be their friend based on criteria.

Another Critiquing instructional task is having students self-assess or peer-assess assignments according to the assignment rubric. This feedback can give students time to revise their assignment before turning it in for a grade while also compelling students to carefully read rubric expectations and utilize their higher-level thinking skills.

Classroom Example Evaluate Level: Critiquing
In-class instruction: Students compared the US election process to the school's student council election.
Assessment: Prior to the school's student council election, the students develop criteria for judging candidates for the position of student council president. After listening to candidates' speeches, students select the candidate that best meets their criteria and defend their decision.

 Level 6: Create

Create

The final level of Bloom's taxonomy is the Create level. At this level learners are organizing information in a new or different way. This stage requires creative thinking. Silva (2008) states that "college students, workers, and citizens must be able to solve multifaceted problems by thinking creatively and generating original ideas from multiple sources of information" (p. 1). The need for creative thinking is also echoed by the Partnership for 21st Century Skills (2011), which considers creativity and innovation to be "some of the most important areas on which to focus CCSS (Common Core State Standards) work. In the 21st century, creativity and innovation skills are central components of college and career readiness" (p. 12).

The Create level has often been misunderstood. Creativity might involve designing a unique product, but it also includes combining various sources of information into a new product (Anderson and Krathwohl, 2001). Through the Create process, students will design a new product *different from the original materials*. According to Facione (2011), "*Creative* or *innovative thinking* [emphasis added] is the kind of thinking that leads to new insights, novel approaches, fresh perspectives, whole new ways of understanding and conceiving of things" (p. 14). This level could include solving a complex real-world problem or testing hypotheses through experimental inquiry. The product could be in the form of a presentation, paper, sculpture, or many other formats. However, "creating" a poster or website does not necessarily mean the task is at the Create level. As with all the Bloom's levels, teachers need to focus on how students are using the content in the class at a particular cognitive level (Maxwell, Stobaugh, & Tassell, 2012). For example, if students "created" a poster or website summarizing one of Shakespeare's plays, the task would be on the Understand level (Summarizing cognitive process). However, if students had to select a book that was at least 100 years old and market it to preteens, this task would require creativity to think about the themes in the text and how they could appeal to students today. At the Create level, students must utilize the skills from lower levels of thinking, particularly the Understand, Analyze, and Evaluate levels, as they seek to examine information and products already produced in order to determine the best way to design their product. At the Create level there are three cognitive processes: Generating, Planning, and Producing.

Create-Level Cognitive Process: Generating

A local community wants to honor the soldiers who have served in the military and positively impacted the community for many years. Community members brainstorm a list of possible ways to do that, including building a commemorative statue, dedicating a park, building a veterans' hospital, holding an annual celebration of veterans, initiating a scholarship fund, and founding a Reserve Officers' Training Corps (ROTC) program in the local schools.

With the Generating cognitive process, the goal is to explore various hypotheses or ideas to address a novel or ill-defined problem. Often decisions or projects are based on quickly selecting one idea, without considering all the alternatives. Generating a novel solution might require examining the problem from another angle. Swartz & Parks (1994) comment, "Generative skills are creative thinking skills: They stretch our thinking and develop our imaginations" (p. 6). Pablo Picasso, an innovative artist, had a similar view: "Computers are useless. They can only give you answers." Creative ideas can lead to new paths.

In school, perhaps the problem is that the hallways are too crowded, causing numerous disciplinary incidents. The administration schedules more teachers to monitor the halls. However, perhaps the administration should consider other options, such as releasing classes at different times or teaching pro-social behaviors to students. Generating involves examining the problem from various angles. Once people understand the various facets of the problem, flexible thinking is necessary to consider new ideas and different viewpoints, whereas close-minded thinking will limit the process. In this idea-generating stage, divergent thinking encourages ideas to emerge that are different from the current thinking about the problem. The ability to propose many solutions to problems is often termed "fluency." Inventor Thomas Edison, who earned 1,093 American patents, said, "To have a great idea, have a lot of them." The ideas should also be varied (flexibility), unique (originality), and detailed (elaboration) (Swartz & Parks, 1994). Judgment is suspended until all possible options are generated. Some ideas might seem impractical, but it is important to collect a variety of novel ideas. Fogarty (1997) suggests the DOVE guidelines to assist with the generating process. "D" refers to students deferring judgment and considering all options. In considering different ideas, "O" represents opting for the outlandish. "V" stands for seeking a vast number of ideas, and "E" means to expand by connecting ideas to other ideas.

There are many instructional tasks on the Generating level, such as the following:

- **Social studies:** Students examine all the different ways to launch an advertising campaign for a new technological device.

- **Language arts:** Students rewrite the ending of a book by brainstorming possible endings or listing various modern-day adaptations to an older text.

- **Science:** Students create hypotheses explaining why the results of an experiment came out a certain way.

- **Math:** Students identify all the possible ways to solve a complex, real-world problem.

Another option is for students to record many different ways to solve a community problem. Each of these creative thinking tasks can be assessed according to criteria. For example, for the book ending, teachers could assess if it represents the ideas of the text but in a modern-day adaptation. Due to the nature of this cognitive process, the assessment must be in an open-ended format.

Classroom Example
Create Level: Generating

In-class instruction:

Students research the role of economics in businesses.

Assessment:

Over the years, the school lunch program has received reduced revenue due to fewer students buying lunches. Brainstorm all the possible reasons for this problem and ways to reverse this trend.

Create-Level Cognitive Process: Planning

The community group reviews possible options to honor local soldiers and considers the criteria: long-term impact, availability of financial resources, and the desire to show community support for the military. Based on these criteria, the group chooses to provide money to the local schools to support an ROTC that would also annually honor the local veterans in a commemorative ceremony. The group then creates a plan with four main steps:

1. *Contact the schools to discuss the prospect of starting an ROTC group.*

2. *If the schools support the idea, identify the financial resources needed to launch and maintain funding for the ROTC.*

3. *Begin fund-raising to obtain the needed financial resources to support the ROTC.*

4. *After the ROTC is established, collaborate yearly with it to plan a commemorative ceremony for veterans in the community.*

For each of the above steps, group members are assigned tasks and completion dates are set.

Anderson and Krathwohl (2001) describe Planning as "devising a solution method that meets a problem's criteria, that is, developing a plan for solving the problem" (p. 87). This Planning process would involve identifying specific tasks to implement the action plan. This is a convergent phase in which the best idea from the Generating phase is selected and a plan of action is formed. First, the problem or issue is clearly identified, understood, and analyzed (Understand/Analyze level). Then, after brainstorming a list of good ideas (Generating), the planners select the best option based on criteria (Critiquing). Paul and Elder (2005) state, "The mind when thinking well must simultaneously both produce and assess, both generate and judge, the products it constructs. Sound thinking requires both imagination and intellectual discipline" (p. 13). Finally, a plan is designed to implement the best solution (Planning). The Planning cognitive process is encouraged by the Partnership for 21st Century Skills (2011), which promotes students' use of their creativity to make real contributions to the fields of study. According to business leaders, the competency that upcoming leaders lack the most is strategic thinking, which hinges on critical thinking skills within the Planning cognitive process (Chartrand, Ishikawa, & Flander, 2009).

The following are examples of school activities at the Planning level:

◆ **Language arts:** Students create an outline to plan their persuasive news article to address a community problem or use graphic organizers to help them organize their thoughts.

- **Science:** Students design a scientific experiment to test an idea.
- **Math:** Students develop a plan to address a complex, real-world math problem.

Sometimes in their planning, students will realize the solution is not correct and need to stop, reverse course, and switch to another idea. Often in open-ended problem-solving, there may be more than one correct plan for accomplishing a goal.

Classroom Example Create Level: Planning
In-class instruction: Students research the role of economics in businesses.
Assessment: Based on the ideas you generated to increase the lunchroom revenue, select the best idea and design a plan for a marketing campaign to increase the percentage of students buying lunches in our school.

Create-Level Cognitive Process: Producing

Two members of the community group visit the principals of the local middle school and high school. The administrators are thrilled at the prospect of starting the ROTC, but register their concern for supporting the program due to limited financial resources. The community members assure the principals that the community would be financially supporting the group on a yearly basis. The principals agree to meet with the district office to discuss the initiative. After all parties agree to move forward, the group begins its fund-raising program. The appropriate ROTC officials are contacted to initiate the program. After about a year of planning, the new ROTC program is launched in the local schools. Local veterans are on hand to celebrate the new program as well as to be honored. A year later, the new ROTC students plan their first commemorative ceremony for local veterans.

Producing is the follow-through of the plan developed in the Planning cognitive process. In the Apply level, a student makes something new by following a procedure. At the Producing level, however, a student must analyze the information (Differentiating, Organizing, and Attributing), brainstorm possibilities to address the question (Generating), select the best option (Critiquing), design a plan to implement a solution (Planning), and then carry out the solution that is different entirely from the original sources (Producing).

All these steps must be followed in a Producing-level task. Many times students "create" products like a brochure. However, they merely use the brochure to list facts on a given topic—a low-level task—rather than giving the brochure an authentic audience or purpose. By contrast, the Producing cognitive level requires complex and deep thinking.

Teachers and schools often conduct action research projects involving all three of the cognitive processes in the Create level by generating solutions to a school problem (Generating), creating an action plan (Planning), and implementing the plan (Producing). For instructional tasks, students can write a research paper, conduct an experiment, collect and analyze poll data, and draft a proposed bill for a school mock congress. Authentic assessments provide ways to create instructional tasks and assessments at this cognitive level. For example, your school is going to start a school television show that will be broadcast to the community and students. Your class is assigned to design a news program. To do this well, extensive research and planning would be important. Researching other news programs and brainstorming ideas for the program (Generating) would prepare for the show. Then the group would prioritize goals for the program and design a plan for launching and maintaining the show (Planning). Finally, the group would begin producing the show (Producing). The benefit of authentic tasks like this is that they replicate the complexities, creativity, and collaboration required in the real world. They nurture skills that employers desire (Partnership for 21st Century Skills, 2011).

Classroom Example Create Level: Producing
In-class instruction:
Students research the role of economics in businesses.
Assessment:
Students implement their marketing campaign plan to increase the percentage of students buying school lunches.

Inquiry and Problem-Solving

Inquiry and problem-solving lessons often address the cognitive processes within the Create level. Problem-solving refers to the step-by-step process of addressing a situation and determining a solution, often while encountering obstacles (Reed, 2000). This process involves generating options, planning a solution to solve the problem, decision-making, and then implementing a solution. One problem-solving model is called design thinking:

- Identify an opportunity: Identify a school or community issue and gather information about the problem.

- Design: Brainstorm solutions to the problem and research the best ideas.

- Prototype: Identify how the solution will work—sketch, build, make a prototype.

- Get feedback: Ask experts to review work and give feedback for improvement.

- Scale and spread: Plan the implementation, which might include work subgroups to accomplish the tasks.

- Present: Present the ideas in an authentic setting, whether via Skype or face to face (Ray, 2012).

These models provide ways for students to structure their thinking to design solutions. This model represents the cognitive processes within the Create level.

Critical thinking also is connected to a movement in education toward inquiry-based or problem-based learning. According to Schamel and Ayres (1992), students learn in a more effective manner when they generate their own questions based on their observations rather than developing a solution to a situation or problem with a predetermined answer. After students identify a question, they identify resources needed, including potential experts. In collaboration with the teacher, students establish the learning target for the project and the assessment. The teacher monitors progress through checking the completion timeline. The students' final project would be an authentic performance task. Many science teachers embrace the active, inquiry-based teaching model where students design a solution to a problem requiring higher levels of cognition. While this model moves away from the rote memorization of scientific concepts, there is supporting evidence that students learn as many basic facts through this model as in a teacher-directed lecture. The positive benefit with this model is that students tend to be able to recall their learning for a longer time (Gabel & National Science Teachers Association, 1994).

Summary

For decades, Benjamin Bloom's cognitive taxonomy has been used by educators throughout the world to classify learning tasks. The recent revisions by Anderson and Krathwohl (2001) produced the six levels Remember, Understand, Apply, Analyze, Evaluate, and Create. Within each level are multiple cognitive processes to further describe the kind of thinking in each level. The levels and cognitive processes provide a frame of reference to examine lessons and assessments and determine the level of thinking expected.

Discuss

◆ Thinking back to your educational experience, what was one instructional task that enhanced your learning about a particular content area? What level on Bloom's taxonomy was the task?

◆ Describe the strategies used by teachers you had who *did* and who *did not* encourage you to think critically. At what level would you classify those strategies?

Take Action

1. Cognitive Domain Planning Tool

   Using the Cognitive Domain Planning Tool (Figure 2.2), list the instructional strategies and formative and summative assessments for a unit of study.

   ◆ How much time do you spend teaching at each of the cognitive levels?

   ◆ Have you found a difference in student learning with the strategies that were taught on the higher levels?

   ◆ What low-level activity or assessment could you remove and what instructional task or assessment could you add to enhance the critical thinking skills in your unit?

2. Bloom's Taxonomy Question Starters

   Using the chart labeled Bloom's Taxonomy Question Starters (Figure 2.3, pages 44–46), reflect on your questioning.

   ◆ Which question stems do you typically use?

   ◆ Which higher-level question stems could you start using?

   ◆ If you use higher-level questions, how does this affect wait time after questioning?

   ◆ If you gave your students this chart, how could they lead the questioning in your class?

   ◆ How could you use this chart to remind yourself to pose higher-level questions?

3. Bloom's Taxonomy Task Prompts

   Using the chart labeled Bloom's Taxonomy Task Prompts (Figure 2.4, pages 47–48), examine the tasks at the various levels.

   ◆ Circle tasks and assessments you use in your instruction that are similar to the task prompts at each level.

   ◆ What are some suggested tasks at the Analyze, Evaluate, and Create levels that you could incorporate into your instruction?

Figure 2.2 **Cognitive Domain Planning Tool**

This tool allows you to examine your current instruction to determine how many of your instruction tasks and assessments for a particular unit are at which level. For a given unit of study, identify the instructional tasks, formative assessments, and summative assessments for each cognitive process.

Cognitive Domain Planning Tool			
Process Categories	Instructional Tasks	Formative Assessments	Summative Assessments
Remember			
1.1 Recognizing			
1.2 Recalling			
Understand			
2.1 Interpreting			
2.2 Exemplifying			
2.3 Classifying			
2.4 Summarizing			
2.5 Inferring			
2.6 Comparing			
2.7 Explaining			
Apply			
3.1 Executing			
3.2 Implementing			
Analyze			
4.1 Differentiating			
4.2 Organizing			
4.3 Attributing			
Evaluate			
5.1 Checking			
5.2 Critiquing			
Create			
6.1 Generating			
6.2 Planning			
6.3 Producing			

Figure 2.3   Bloom's Taxonomy Question Starters

Bloom's Taxonomy Question Starters	
Remembering	
Recognizing	Who, what, when, and where questions when students must select the answer ♦ For example, "Government by the people would describe which type of government—democracy or monarchy?"
Recalling	Who, what, when, and where questions when the student must recall the answer from memory ♦ For example, "Government by the people would describe which type of government?" ♦ Repeat back …
Understand	
Interpreting	♦ Can you say that in a different way? ♦ What does this mean? ♦ How would you describe _____ to another person? ♦ Define in your own words _____. ♦ Can you describe that picture?
Exemplifying	♦ What is another example of _____? ♦ What is an example of _____ in your life?
Classifying	♦ What is _____ an example of? ♦ How might you sort _____ into groups or categories? ♦ What rules or characteristics have been used to form the groups or categories?
Summarizing	♦ What is the main idea of the reading? ♦ Can you summarize what you just said? ♦ What is another title for this reading?
Inferring	♦ What are the implications of _____? ♦ Why did the author do _____? ♦ What can you conclude from the evidence or pieces of information? ♦ In this context, what was intended by saying/doing that? ♦ How is this connected to _____? ♦ What do you think will probably happen next? ♦ What is the relationship between _____ and _____?
Comparing	♦ How is _____ like _____? ♦ Why is _____ like _____? ♦ Can you distinguish between _____ and _____? ♦ How are _____ and _____ different? ♦ Describe the differences between _____ and _____.

(continued)

Bloom's Taxonomy Question Starters

Explaining	◆ Based on the information so far, what will happen next? ◆ Predict the effects or implications of _____. ◆ Describe what might have caused this to happen. ◆ How would you change _____?
Apply	
Executing	◆ Using the taught procedure, how would you solve this problem? ◆ How can you use this procedure in some other instance?
Implementing	◆ Which procedure would you use to solve this problem? ◆ What is another way you could arrive at the solution?
Analyze	
Differentiating	◆ What information do you need to solve this problem or approach this task? ◆ Describe what facts in the informational source support _____. ◆ Which piece of evidence or information is most important to consider? ◆ What evidence have you got to back that up?
Organizing	◆ What familiar pattern do you notice? ◆ How could you organize or combine these ideas? ◆ How would you combine, or organize, _____ and _____?
Attributing	◆ Which is fact, opinion, or inference? ◆ What are the motives behind _____? ◆ What are the reasons for both perspectives? ◆ How would this look from the viewpoint of _____? ◆ What is the point of view of the author? ◆ What are the other viewpoints? ◆ What assumptions must we make to accept that conclusion? ◆ Should we accept these assumptions or question them? ◆ What are other ways of looking at this issue? ◆ Would you rather be _____ or _____? Why? ◆ Would you like to be _____? Why or why not? ◆ What is your opinion on _____? What evidence do you have to support your opinion?

(continued)

Bloom's Taxonomy Question Starters	
Evaluate	
Checking	◆ How could we verify that was true? ◆ Is that always true? ◆ Why do you believe that? ◆ How strong are those arguments? ◆ Is there a defect in any of the data or evidence provided? ◆ How credible is that claim? ◆ What are the reasons for the claim? ◆ What is your basis for saying that? ◆ Do the conclusions follow the reasoning? ◆ How can we check to see if this argument is accurate? ◆ What additional information do we need to resolve this question? ◆ What are the strengths and weaknesses of this piece of evidence?
Critiquing	◆ Appraise, critique, judge, or evaluate _____. Support your appraisal, critique, judgment, or evaluation with evidence. ◆ Why do you suppose that is good? ◆ Is this _____ successful? What evidence do you have to support your opinion? ◆ Could _____ be better? Why or why not? ◆ Which is better? Why? ◆ How would you rate or judge _____? ◆ What choice would you have made? Support your position. ◆ What are the arguments pro and con? ◆ What are the advantages or disadvantages of _____? ◆ Take a position on _____ and justify, support, defend, or prove your position. ◆ Why do you think that was the right answer or solution? ◆ Are there any undesirable consequences that we can and should foresee? ◆ What are the consequences of doing things that way? ◆ Explain what criteria you would use to evaluate which is the best option. ◆ What is the most (least) important part? ◆ How effective is _____?
Create	
Generating	◆ What are some alternatives to solving this problem that we haven't yet explored? ◆ For this problem, what do you think would happen if _____? Why?
Planning	◆ What steps would you take to implement your plan?
Producing	◆ What product would best achieve the desired result?

Source: Some items adapted from Stanley (2006) and Stiggins, Arter, Chappuis, & Chappuis (2004).

Figure 2.4 **Bloom's Taxonomy Task Prompts**

Bloom's Taxonomy Task Prompts	
Remembering	
Recognizing	◆ Match the word and definition. ◆ Using a word bank, label a diagram.
Recalling	◆ Make a list of all the information you remember. ◆ Answer fact-based questions in a typical *Jeopardy* game.
Understand	
Interpreting	◆ Explain the concepts studied to a student who has never heard of this before. ◆ Make a list of the main ideas in the passage. ◆ Draw a picture or symbol to represent _____. ◆ Cut out pictures that represent _____. ◆ Create a hand motion to symbolize _____. ◆ In your own words, describe _____. ◆ Draw a cartoon showing the sequence of events.
Exemplifying	◆ Identify another example of _____. ◆ Explain how this information applies to your life. ◆ Provide an example of _____.
Classifying	◆ Group the key words into clusters of similar ideas. ◆ Classify the following _____ into categories.
Summarizing	◆ Write a news report summarizing _____. ◆ Create an outline of _____.
Inferring	◆ Create an analogy for _____. ◆ Create a metaphor for _____. ◆ Describe the relationship between _____ and _____. ◆ Identify ways in which one action could positive and negatively impact other variables.
Comparing	◆ Compare _____ and _____ based on the following elements: _____.
Explaining	◆ Create a cause-and-effect diagram. ◆ If _____ happens, what might happen? ◆ Explain how alternative actions might impact _____.
Apply	
Executing	◆ Determine the longitude and latitude of a city on a map. ◆ After learning to create a graph or table, design a table.
Implementing	◆ Write a letter of complaint to a company. ◆ After collecting survey data, select the best way to show the data.

(continued)

Bloom's Taxonomy Task Prompts	
Analyze	
Differentiating	◆ Mark out any irrelevant information in the problem or data set.
Organizing	◆ Create a way to organize the data in order to draw meaningful conclusions. ◆ Combine or organize the information in a meaningful way. ◆ Organize the information provided in appropriate categories. ◆ Put the information into a flowchart or a diagram. ◆ Create a chart or graph to show _____.
Attributing	◆ Identify the pros and cons of _____. ◆ Describe your own biases regarding this idea. ◆ Conduct a debate about an issue.
Evaluate	
Checking	◆ Examine the source and determine if it would be appropriate to support an argument. ◆ For the given source, identify the weaknesses and strengths. ◆ Review each source cited to determine the quality of information and evidence presented. ◆ Identify the claim and the supporting evidence. ◆ Highlight unsupported claims.
Critiquing	◆ Select the best option for the given problem or idea based on criteria (e.g., feasibility, consequences). ◆ Prioritize the solutions to the problem. ◆ Put in order of importance the key actions. ◆ Evaluate according to criteria the best _____. ◆ Identify the criteria to measure success. ◆ Determine the costs and benefits for each given solution. ◆ Evaluate a classmate's work based on rubric criteria. ◆ Determine the best course of action or decision based on a set of criteria.
Create	
Generating	◆ Create a list of all the possible solutions for _____ (a real-world problem). ◆ What would change if _____? ◆ Invent a solution for _____. ◆ Formulate a hypothesis for _____. ◆ Design a survey to _____.
Planning	◆ Create a plan to solve a problem over time. ◆ Draw up a plan to show how your idea will work.
Producing	◆ Deliver a presidential speech outlining a plan to address a real-world problem. ◆ Design a website to persuade your community to take action on an environmental issue.

Misconceptions, Challenges, and a Solution

The world we have created is a product of our thinking; it cannot be changed without changing our thinking.

—Albert Einstein

"Critical thinking" is a term often used, but sometimes misunderstood, leading to many misconceptions among educators. Due to the misunderstanding about higher-level thinking, teachers sometimes use lower-level assessments and instructional tasks. However, there is a solution! By using interpretive exercises, teachers can design instructional tasks and assessments at higher levels of cognitive complexity. This chapter will address critical thinking misconceptions, consider the challenges infusing cognitively engaging tasks and assessments, and then present a solution.

Misconceptions

Misconceptions about Bloom's cognitive taxonomy are rampant. Eleven misconceptions will be addressed here. Due to these confusions, many teachers believe they are providing critical thinking tasks when, in reality, they are not. By recognizing these common misunderstandings, teachers can plan more appropriate instructional tasks and assessments for their students.

#1: Critical Thinking Assessments Used Multiple Times

As an administrator, I had my staff work together to revise assessments. After working with the teachers in one content area to get their summative assessment revised, I was thrilled that their work incorporated deep-thinking processes. The day before the test, I was doing some routine walk-through visits in the classrooms. I noticed one of the teachers had the test in hand and was asking the test questions to prepare students for the next day's assessment. The class then discussed the answers to the high-level questions. As I returned to my office, I realized that I had not clearly communicated what critical thinking meant. The questions the teacher asked on the review day were high-level. However, if the teacher used those same questions the next day, then students would just be remembering the answers and not thinking critically, because they would already know the answers thanks to the previous day's discussion.

While I was conducting training for another school, a school counselor had an epiphany and said, "So you mean that we really don't know if the test is high-level simply by looking at the questions." She was correct. The items on the test might be high-level, but if the teacher has already discussed the items in class before the test, then the test would represent the lowest level on Bloom's taxonomy, the Remember level. Once the answer to a high-level question is discussed, the assessment item functions as a memorized answer for future testing purposes. After the answers to a critical thinking question have been discussed, different questions have to be constructed for further assessments in order to maintain the high level of cognitive complexity.

#2: Teachers Using High-Level Bloom's Words

In their desperation to get help in understanding Bloom's work, some teachers search the Internet and locate lists of verbs that align to each level. Or, they purchase a Bloom's flip chart for help. I affectionately call these people "Bloom's Flip Chart Addicts." While the flip charts and verb charts can be helpful resources, teachers who do not understand the premise of Bloom's framework simply select a word from one of the higher levels of the framework and plunk it into an instructional objective or assessment—for example, "Synthesize the passage and explain who is the main character." Using a high-level verb like "synthesize" does not mean the question automatically becomes a high-level assessment item. The teacher must consider what level of thinking is being requested. In this case, the student is most likely identifying the main character; if the passage is new to the student, then the question would be on an Understand level.

Due to this confusion, I recommend using the lists of verbs for each Bloom's level carefully, if at all. The word "explain" can be used appropriately on several different levels of Bloom's taxonomy. For example, "Explain in your own words the definition of a *chemical solution*" is an Understand-level task, whereas "Explain what is the best solution for solving the recycling problem in our neighborhood" could be on the Create level. Many teachers misunderstand these lists, so I rarely use them. Instead, one strategy I recommend for teachers is examining the response time for students. Most of the time, students can respond to low-level questions quickly, whereas tasks or questions at the Analyzing level and above are almost impossible to answer orally. The complexity of Analyze-, Evaluate-, and Create-level tasks requires students to read the question several times, often put thoughts on paper, and perhaps even do some research before deriving a solution.

#3: Difficult Tasks Are High-Level Thinking Tasks

I am terrible at the game Trivial Pursuit. I depend on technology to help me remember trivia information. All the questions in Trivial Pursuit and *Jeopardy* games are low-level questions, on the Remember level, but they would be considered difficult. For example, to name a river in South Africa that you heard mentioned once on television, without the use of any resources, would be a difficult question for most people, but it is a fact and does not require higher-level thinking processes. Perhaps you know people who have a phenomenal memory but lack the ability to think critically. When selecting instructional tasks and assessments, teachers need to assess at what level on Bloom's taxonomy students will process the information. The level of difficulty and the level of thinking processes are different entities.

#4: Lessons Focus on Technology or Creative Arts Instead of the Thinking Levels of the Content

Teachers often incorporate technology or art into their assessments. When this happens, the assessment is often measuring two elements: technology use or creative arts *and* content. For example, a first-year teacher gave me a lesson plan with the objective, "Students will be able to create a Power-Point presentation on George Washington." The teacher thought that this assignment was on the Create level of Bloom's taxonomy. When we met before the lesson, I asked her what exactly students would be doing when they designed the presentation. She said that students would be looking up information online about Washington and summarizing the key events of his administration. In regard to students' thinking about the social studies content, her assessment fit on the Understanding level because they were summarizing. She also had a secondary purpose to utilize the technology. In this case, because students had already designed PowerPoint presentations before, they were applying that skill to this assignment. Therefore, the technology objective for this task would be classified on the Apply level, whereas the social studies content was on the Understanding level. This discrepancy often happens with creative art tasks like designing a mural or dramatic skit.

Most assessments are classified in regard to thinking using the content, unless of course the class focus is on technology use or creative arts. You need to consider your students' use of technology and artistic skills as separate dimensions when assessing. Also, remember that the technology or creative art task may be on a different cognitive level than the thinking about the content in the task. Keep your focus on the content!

#5: Teachers Believe the Level of Thinking Is the Same for All Students

A teacher might design an assignment on one of the higher levels of Bloom's taxonomy and yet still have students turn in work at various levels on the taxonomy. For example, if the assignment was to create a storybook for elementary students about an environmental issue in the community, some students would design an original story and characters about a real community issue. However, other students might struggle and produce a story that mimics one they had read earlier. Thus, the task was on a high level, but the work produced was on various levels: the students who created the novel story would be working at the Create level, whereas those who imitated a story already written would be on a much lower level.

#6: Student Thinking Is Best Assessed Through Oral Questioning

When I was conducting a school training, the teachers explained that the district office the next day would be conducting walk-through observations in the school looking for higher-level thinking instruction. The teachers were told that the observers would be recording only what was said by the teacher. I commented to the principal that this would not give a fair picture of the level of thinking in the school because often the highest levels of thinking are assessed by assignments and tasks with details recorded on paper or technology. With higher levels of cognitive processing, students need time to think. In fact, students might work several days or more to produce a product at the Create level.

#7: Multiple-Choice Assessments Demand Low-Level Thinking; Writing Tasks Require High-Level Thinking

Assessment formats can also bridge across several Bloom's levels. Another misconception is that multiple-choice questions can assess only basic knowledge. Actually, multiple-choice questions can assess understandings on the Remember, Understand, Apply, and Analyze levels. For example, high-level thinking multiple-choice questions can ask students to identify the best conclusion from a data set. Many testing companies use multiple-choice questions to assess students' higher-level thinking due to the ability to efficiently score student responses.

Some teachers think that a question that requires an open-ended response is automatically a higher-level item. However, some essay prompts simply require students to produce facts. Writing can be a lower-level task if it does not call forth new ideas or ideas organized in a new way. Thus, it is important to examine the open-ended response prompt to ensure it requires higher levels of thinking. If the teacher wants to assess lower levels of thinking, a selected-response assessment format provides a quick and efficient way to assess this knowledge. Since open-ended questions are time-consuming to score, teachers should reserve open-ended questions to address the higher levels of thinking in Bloom's taxonomy. For example, "Which political candidate is the best choice for our state? Why?"

#8: Bloom's Tasks Do Not Match Standards or Student Needs

While Bloom's taxonomy defines the levels, the point is to increase the level of thinking. Sometimes educators disagree at what level to categorize the instructional task or assessment. Essentially, teachers should focus on developing higher-level instructional experiences and not spend time arguing about the Bloom's levels for tasks and assessments.

With the pressure to incorporate higher-level processes, sometimes teachers select a Bloom's level to work toward that might not be a good fit with the standard they are teaching. For example, a teacher is teaching a new skill: how to add fractions. To incorporate higher-level thinking, the teacher determines that instruction will be on the Create level. However, to learn the skill, students really need practice at the Apply level. After they master the skill, it might be appropriate for students to propose, design, and implement a Create-level task.

It is not necessary to teach and assess at the highest level of Bloom's taxonomy, the Create level, in order to attain every content standard. Completing Create-level tasks often requires a significant amount of time. Given the numerous standards expected to be taught, it probably is not possible to have a Create-level task for each concept. However, Create-level tasks can be selectively planned and show a culminating performance of students' knowledge and abilities.

When deciding at what level to teach to, teachers should ascertain the students' background knowledge. It is important that teachers build on the students' prior knowledge. If students already have a strong understanding of the content, challenging students to Analyze, Evaluate, or Create would stretch their thinking. However, some classes may feel overwhelmed when assigned a Create-level task. Having students regularly develop their thinking on Analyze- and Evaluate-level tasks can build up their skills, preparing them to complete a Create-level task.

Some subjects seem to lend themselves easily to the higher levels. For example, in language arts classes, students do quite a bit of original writing that is on the Create level. Other classes are heavily embedded with skills to teach; in math, for example, quite a bit of instruction is on the Apply level.

#9: Young Students Cannot Complete Higher-Level Tasks

Some consider that higher-level thinking tasks are appropriate only for high school and college students. However, high-level thinking tasks are suitable for all ages. In fact, if students in primary grades do not master cognitive skills like comparing, classifying, sequencing, and predicting, they will rarely achieve grade-level performance in reading comprehension and independent learning (Siegler, 1998). Therefore, young students need to be taught thinking skills in order for them to successfully understand content.

#10: Some Educators Have False Assumptions on How Students Learn

Paul & Elder (2007) state that some teachers design lessons based on false assumptions, including the following:

1. Lecture content can be absorbed with minimal intellectual engagement on the part of the students.

2. Students can learn important content without much intellectual work.

3. Memorization is the key to learning, so that students need to store up lots of information that they can use later when they need it.

If instruction predominantly consists of students memorizing information, they will forget a large amount of their learning. In research measuring student thinking, teachers whose lessons centered on teaching facts or specific problem types for a test had students who did not develop deep conceptual understandings or were unable to apply their learning to different circumstances (Shepard, Hammerness, Darling-Hammond, & Rust, 2005). When students engage in deep processing of content, it leads to greater transfer of the knowledge into long-term memory and content mastery. Paul and Elder (2007) state, "The only capacity we can use to learn is human thinking. If we think well while learning, we learn well. If we think poorly while learning, we learn poorly" (p. 8). Thus, in order to learn in any content area, students must think critically by evaluating and analyzing the content in that discipline. By thinking at a deep level, students learn to internalize the content and make it meaningful to them. By structuring learning experiences around high-level thinking and content engagement, teachers help their students become knowledge producers instead of simply knowledge consumers. According to Paul and Elder (2007),

> Educated persons function differently from uneducated persons. They are able to enter and intellectually empathize with alternate ways of looking at things. They change their minds when evidence or reasoning require it. They are able to internalize important concepts within a discipline and

inter-relate those concepts with other important concepts both within and among disciplines. They are able to reason well to think their way through complex problems. If students are to become educated persons, teachers must place thinking at the heart of the curriculum; they must require students to actively work ideas into their thinking using their thinking. (p. 9)

In essence, deep thinking is inseparable from lifelong learning.

#11: High-Level Tasks Are for Gifted Students

Sometimes teachers will document on their lesson plan that gifted students will receive higher-order thinking questions as an adaptation. On the other end of the spectrum, learners who seem to be less capable are given fill-in-the-blank worksheets requiring only low levels of thinking. Unless all students gain access to cognitively engaging tasks, the achievement gap will continue to widen (Torff, 2011). President Barack Obama has stated that every student will graduate from high school ready for college and a career (U.S. Department of Education, 2010). For this to happen, all students must be exposed to critical thinking tasks.

However, not all students get equal access to critical thinking tasks. Not surprisingly, a more significant focus on high-level critical thinking activities has been found in upper-track classes (Raudenbush, Rowan, & Cheong, 1993). Teachers in minority schools often support reducing the availability of critical thinking tasks for disadvantaged students (Torff, 2005, 2006, 2008). These teachers have good intentions, believing that the higher-level tasks will frustrate students. However, evidence shows that disadvantaged students along with advantaged students benefit from cognitively engaging curriculum (Zohar & Dori, 2003; Pogrow, 1990, 1994). Teachers can harm students by underestimating their abilities. Teachers may assume that students with varying skills and cultural experiences are incapable of cognitively complex tasks. Instead, teachers should cultivate a growth mind-set that allows them to see all students as having potential to learn (Dweck, 2006; Olson, 2009). Student potential should be viewed as an iceberg, with most of the children's aptitudes concealed from view (Tomlinson & Javius, 2012). With a supportive environment and high expectations, these abilities will be revealed. If disadvantaged students are deprived of cognitively complex tasks, they will fall further behind in a repetitive cycle.

If all students are to reach high levels of learning, then we cannot continue to provide critical thinking activities just to our advanced students. In our democracy, schools are charged with providing a quality education for all students. If we fail to offer opportunities for all students to engage in complex thinking, we fail to equip them with the tools to be successful. Critical thinking activities help all students develop deeper understandings of concepts (Paul & Elder, 2007).

Moore and Stanley (2010) compare thinking to sports. Any person can learn to be better at critical thinking if given enough time and practice. When students initially work on critical thinking tasks, they need modeling and practice, just as with any other skill students learn. They need to be coached on strategies to approach the task and given graphic organizers to construct their thoughts. Without such support, students may become overwhelmed. Teachers should not get frustrated if at first students do not receive high marks on cognitively complex assignments. Practice and feedback will improve students' abilities. We all have seen teachers who required students to produce work that engaged higher-level thinking skills. Those teachers raised the level of expectations, modeled thinking strategies, provided many developmentally appropriate opportunities for students to practice their thinking skills, offered encouragement and constructive feedback, and found students could reach high levels of thinking.

Challenges

The need for embedding critical thinking tasks into the curriculum is clear. However, there are several challenges to increasing the quantity of critical thinking tasks in classrooms. Through awareness of these challenges, educators can be prepared for obstacles they may encounter as they try to implement a cognitively complex curriculum.

Familiarity and Comfort with Low-Level Tasks and Assessments

Often, teachers create assessments at a Remember level, the lowest level of thinking in Bloom's taxonomy. In a research study of more than 8,800 test questions created by elementary and high school teachers, Fleming and Chambers (1983) found that nearly 80 percent were at the Remember level. Almost ten years later, a national representative survey found similar results. Through content analysis, Madaus, West, Harmon, Lomax, and Viator (1992) determined that only 3 percent of assessment items on tests represented high-level conceptual knowledge and only about 5 percent of the total items sampled assessed higher-level thinking skills of any type. The other 95 percent of items sampled involved the low-level skills of recalling information, calculating, and using formulas to solve routine problems similar to problems worked in the textbook or in class. These results are echoed by Goodlad (2004), who reported that 90 percent of the time in schools, teachers relayed information to students from a textbook and then assessed them on their memorization of this information.

With a large portion of teacher-designed tests assessing at a low level, students may think that education is more about memorizing facts than thinking deeply to develop conceptual understandings. Since students typically perform better on low-level thinking items, teachers may presume that their students are more capable than they are because students were not expected to think at high levels. However, when students are called upon to use high-level processes on state and national assessments, those who have not regularly employed these thinking skills will be unprepared.

As a new principal, I was aware that my school's math scores were relatively low in comparison to the scores in other academic areas. In one math classroom, I noticed that students were completing all the formula-type questions, which were on the Apply level using the Executing cognitive process. Students were not using the math skills required in the kinds of real-world word problems that were included on the state assessment. This misalignment was causing our students to be unprepared for the state assessment. The math teachers collaboratively revised their assessments and instructional tasks to include more real-world problems that required critical thinking and problem-solving. Their hard work over the course of three years led to a 32 percent increase on the state assessment scores. To prepare students appropriately for state assessments as well as life, teachers must develop classroom assessments with high levels of cognitive complexity.

Lack of Understanding of Bloom's Taxonomy

The honest fact is that teachers struggle to create assessment items because they lack the necessary understanding of Bloom's taxonomy and the strategies to increase the critical thinking level of assessments. During their undergraduate years, education majors face a wealth of information that must be learned, from classroom management to lesson planning. Designing high-level assessments is often taught, but might not be considered the most critical part of an undergraduate teacher candidate's program. During their first years as a teacher, in professional learning communities and through professional development, beginning teachers might receive additional training to refine their skills in developing high-level tasks and assessments. However, because many teachers still feel unsure about their assessment-designing skills, they rely on textbook questions or other assessment item banks which may or may not provide cognitively complex assessments.

With the thorough descriptions in this book of the Bloom's levels and the examples in subsequent chapters, the hope is you will be able to identify the different levels of thinking and design instructional tasks and assessments that require your students to use their critical thinking skills.

More Time

Unfortunately, assessment items with high cognitive demand take a long time to create. The process takes much longer than for low-level questions because teachers must create new situations in which students can apply their knowledge. In addition, it takes students longer to answer cognitively complex assessment items because more thinking and processing time is required. Teachers who incorporate higher-level assessments often reduce the number of items on the tests because of the time it takes for students to answer questions.

To mitigate this difficulty, teachers can incorporate interpretive items into their assessments. Interpretative items are a way to increase the level of cognitive complexity of the instructional tasks and assessments by incorporating graphics, scenarios, and quotes.

A Solution: Interpretive Exercises

As educators search for ways to increase the level of thinking in their instructional tasks and assessments to meet the demands of the Common Core State Standards for students to engage in high-level thinking skills, one approach is through embedding interpretive exercises. Nitko and Brookhart (2011) define interpretive exercises as "items or assessment tasks that require the student to use reading material, graphs, tables, pictures, or other material to answer the items" (p. 505). Interpretive exercises begin with introductory materials like graphics, quotes, or scenarios. Students then are asked to examine the introductory materials and use them to complete the instructional task or assessment. In the interpretive exercise example below, a scenario is provided about a candidate wanting to run for the U.S. presidency. In order for students to complete this assessment, they would need to know the

Figure 3.1 **Interpretive Exercise Example**

Susan May's friends are urging her to run for president. She is a forty-year-old teacher from Dallas, Texas. Susan has lived in Texas for the past twenty years but was born and raised in Paris, France. Her parents are French citizens. At the age of twenty she moved to attend Texas A&M University. While in Texas, she became an American citizen. Based only on the information provided, what would prevent Susan from being eligible to run for president at this point in her life?

   a. Susan is a woman.

   b. Susan is forty years old.

   c. Susan has not lived in the United States her whole life.

   d. Susan was not born a U.S. citizen.

   e. None of the above

qualifications for running for the presidency and then scrutinize the scenario provided to determine which of the answer choices is correct.

Interpretive exercises are most often incorporated into forced-choice assessments like multiple-choice questions or an extended response like short answers or essays. In some cases, the interpretive exercises can be the stimulus for students to create projects or products. The many advantages of interpretive exercises are discussed below. In subsequent chapters, numerous examples will be provided in a variety of assessment formats and subject areas.

Assessing Higher-Level Thinking Skills

Interpretive exercises provide numerous advantages; however, the main benefit is that they access higher cognitive levels. In such an exercise, as discussed before, students must encounter a novel problem or situation that requires them to assess the situation and derive an acceptable solution by using both their knowledge of the relevant subject matter and their reasoning skills. By using interpretive materials like graphs, pictures, or reading passages that students have not viewed previously, students are assessed at a higher cognitive level on the new task (Gronlund, 1981; Mehrens & Lehmann, 1984; Nitko 1983).

To answer an interpretive exercise, first students must understand the interpretive materials. Second, students must understand the question or task. They must then identify and access the background information that can help them interpret the new materials. Students must make connections between introductory materials provided and their prior knowledge, which might include facts and terms to answer the question. Finally, students will complete the task, such as identifying the best hypothesis for the data provided, identifying the most important element in a piece of writing that needs to be revised, or evaluating which historical photograph best represents the time period.

Using interpretive materials can assess complex thinking skills such as reading ability, comprehension, mathematical thinking, problem-solving, writing skill, and graph and table interpretation (Haladyna, Downing, & Rodriguez, 2002; Hale & Astolfi, 2011). Interpretive exercises can also assess skills such as recognizing assumptions, identifying valid conclusions, interpreting relationships, differentiating between relevant and irrelevant information, and drawing inferences from reading (Hale & Astolfi, 2011). These exercises provide situations for students to employ their problem-solving skills as they identify problems; select which principles, generalizations, or criteria are relevant to interpreting the information; and utilize critical thinking skills to answer the question. Haladyna, Downing, and Rodriguez (2002) note that interpretive materials are often used in large-scale assessments primarily due to their ability to capture students' thinking processes with great fidelity.

Establishing a Frame of Reference

Students come to assessment experiences with a variety of prior knowledge and experience. An assessment item that uses interpretive materials provides the necessary background information that can be used to think about the content in a new way (Hale & Astolfi, 2011).

Including Multistep Questions

In interpretive exercises, several questions can be based on the same introductory material. Often a series of assessment items based on introductory material can tap greater skills depth and breadth (Hale & Astolfi, 2011; Wainer & Kiely, 1987). Gronlund (2006) agrees: "Complex learning outcomes can frequently be more effectively measured by basing a series of test items on a common selection of introductory material" (p. 103). If the introductory material for an interpretive exercise includes several documents or a data set, several questions or tasks could be crafted to assess several concepts or skills or even varying levels of abilities.

Scoring and Reliability

Another benefit of interpretive exercises is that they can be paired with selected-response questions. Multiple-choice questions have gained a negative reputation as being capable only of assessing factual recall (e.g., vocabulary). However, well-written multiple-choice questions have the potential to assess higher-level thinking skills. Interpretive exercises paired with multiple-choice questions are a more efficient way to assess high-level skills compared to performance assessment. In less time, teachers can assess students' conceptual understanding about a broad range of topics. Such exercises can also be quickly scored due to the possibility of using a selected-response format. And unlike open-ended questions, these items can be objectively scored (Suskie, 2009).

Increasing Student Interest

Often students who have no idea how to answer a question will give up immediately. With interpretative materials, these students have something to examine and spur their thinking. The introductory information with text or graphics gives students something to initially spark their thinking. Additionally, interpretive materials can simulate real-world experiences as they ask students to analyze passages, draw conclusions from data charts, or examine a political cartoon. These applications of knowledge are more interesting than simply recalling information students have been told to memorize.

Aligning to Standards

In some cases it is nearly impossible to align to a standard without using interpretive materials. For example, if students are expected to apply their knowledge of math principles in real-world situations, then students must encounter a real-world situation. In English, to analyze the setting of text, students would need to read a passage from a new text to evaluate it. To determine if students can read a map, students need a map to analyze.

Simulating State and National Assessment Questions

Finally, these types of interpretive questions exist on state and national assessments. Using interpretive materials in class prepares students for the state and national assessments. For example, in 2011, Kentucky launched a new state assessment, Kentucky Performance Rating for Educational Progress (K-PREP). Samples of assessment items for the norm-referenced portion of the test were released. In this document there are multiple examples of interpretive exercises incorporating graphics, scenarios, and passages (Kentucky Department of Education, 2011).

Summary

Despite the misconceptions and challenges, there are many ways to include critical thinking in tasks and assessments. Interpretive materials provide a way to infuse critical thinking skills into the curriculum. Exercises using graphics, scenarios, and quotes can help teachers meet the challenge of creating high-level tasks and assessments. Interpretive materials require students to utilize their higher-level thinking skills. The use of such exercises in class prepares students for state and national assessments, which already embed interpretive materials. The next three chapters will explain various types of interpretive exercises using visuals, quotes, and scenarios while providing numerous examples of instructional tasks and assessments from a variety of content areas.

Discuss

- ◆ Which of the misconceptions in this chapter did you believe?
- ◆ Now that you have learned about the misconceptions, what changes do you need to make in your current practices?
- ◆ What are other misconceptions about cognitive complexity?
- ◆ How are schools perpetuating these misconceptions?

- Where have you seen interpretive exercises?

- How do you think interpretive exercises can help you in your classroom?

Take Action

- Review your instructional tasks and assessments. Do you currently use interpretive exercises?

- Search the Internet or company testing materials. What are some examples of interpretive materials?

Interpretive Exercises: Scenarios and Real-World Applications

One cannot be a good learner and a poor thinker.
—Richard Paul and Linda Elder

One way to create interpretive exercises is through the use of scenarios and real-world applications of students' knowledge. By including new introductory materials, tasks and assessments will move beyond the Remember level on Bloom's taxonomy to increasing levels of cognitive complexity. Scenarios, real-world examples, and authentic tasks are a way to infuse deep cognitive thinking into lessons and assessments in an engaging context.

This chapter will describe how using scenarios, real-world examples, and authentic tasks can increase high-level thinking. Suggestions for constructing instructional tasks and assessments using such interpretive items are identified, followed by examples from several content areas.

Types of Real-World Applications

This chapter presents three ways to incorporate interpretive exercises into lessons and assessments: scenarios, real-world examples, and authentic tasks. A description and the benefits of each are included in this section.

Scenarios

A scenario is a sequence of events or a fictional description of an action or events. Scenarios provide a way of assessing students' application of knowledge in a simulated context. Scenarios are already used in many professional arenas to assess knowledge. Students studying to be nurses read situations or case studies and decide on the best course of action. In law schools, future lawyers identify the issues at stake in a scenario and determine the best way to proceed in the given situation. Perhaps even in your undergraduate teacher education program or state licensure test you were presented with classroom management situations and asked to determine the best way to handle the situation. A scenario example for a social studies class is provided below.

Example

Mr. Spinks's class is creating a list of ways to describe the location of his classroom. Which of these descriptions states the absolute location of the classroom?

a. across the street from the post office

b. 46° N, 123° W

c. the first room on the left

d. three miles north of Portland, Oregon

In this scenario, students must know the definition of "absolute location" and determine which of the answer choices provides the absolute location of the classroom.

When simulations are too expensive or too time-consuming, scenarios provide an easier way to assess thinking in a similar context while maintaining high-level thinking. Scenarios are thus often used on state and national assessments. The Programme for International Student Assessment (PISA) measured fifteen-year-old students' ability to apply math and science concepts in real-world scenarios. In these assessments, U.S. students were among the lowest performers (Lemke et al., 2004). If teachers embed scenarios into their instruction and assessments, students will be better prepared to apply their knowledge on state and national assessments. For classroom instruction and assessments, scenarios can be complex, like a case study with lots of information to comprehend and analyze, or less complicated, like the absolute location example.

Real-World Examples

Real-world examples move beyond the simulated context to provide direct connections between the content and authentic situations. Through real-world instances, students become aware of the extension of their learning in realistic circumstances. In the world and history are examples of concepts that align to content in the curriculum. Unlike fictional scenarios, real-world examples are actual instances that provide a way for students to see the content applied in a meaningful, real way. Real-world situations provide a perfect opportunity for teachers to showcase how student learning applies to contexts outside of school. Additionally, real examples from the students' local community and those that relate to their interests can pique student attention in the topic studied. Below is a real-world example for a business or social studies class.

Example

In 2007, Apple sold about 1 million iPhones. In 2011, about 71 million iPhones were sold.

A. Describe the different marketing techniques Apple is using compared to other companies to increase sales.

_____

_____

B. If Apple wants to continue to be successful, what are two marketing changes that must be made within the next ten years?

_____

_____

In this example, students use their knowledge of marketing to analyze and suggest changes to marketing techniques. As shown in this situation, real-world situations can appeal to students' interest.

Authentic Tasks

Another way to incorporate relevant learning experiences is through designing authentic tasks. While real-world examples connect to historical or current-day applications of the content, authentic tasks simulate job challenges, requiring research and multiple steps to create the solution or product. As the Partnership for 21st Century Skills (2011) states,

> As educators pursue CCSS (Common Core State Standards) alignment, then, it is crucial to design curricula and assessment systems that emphasize authentic real-world problems, engage students in inquiry and exploration and provide opportunities for students to apply what they know in meaningful ways. (p. 10)

Authentic tasks align to 21st-century skills, supporting student-centered approaches with problem-based learning and project-based learning. Through these experiences, students learn to collaborate while working on authentic problems that often positively impact the community (Rotherham & Willingham, 2009). Local business and community partners are a rich source of real-world problems that can be incorporated into an authentic task. Whether the issue is increasing the level of recycling, helping the police to stop graffiti, or designing a web page for a local business, students can devise ways to address the problem and propose realistic solutions. Students will be more motivated to engage in the task due to the real-world context. In addition, students can learn important skills to transfer to various careers, addressing the emphasis in the Common Core State Standards on college and career readiness.

When I was an administrator, my school's writing scores were low. The teachers were diligently working to improve students' writing abilities. I knew that I needed to do more to support the program, so I proposed starting an editorial board. Students who were good writers were selected to serve on this board. I told the student group that our main goal was to encourage student writing. When the editorial board met, the members read submissions by their peers, evaluating them based on the qualities of good writing. The board then selected a piece of writing to profile each week. The selected authors were acknowledged on the school's public address system, and their writing was showcased in our front hall. Visitors enjoyed reading their writing, and the students loved the attention. During editorial board meetings, I was amazed at the conversations among members as they critiqued the submitted work. They brought up points about focus, voice, and grammar. These students serving on the editorial board were doing a real-world job. With authentic tasks, the role of the students shifts from a passive role to assuming a real-world role such as a historian, sports analyst, scientist, or literary critic.

Authentic tasks also provide a way for students to demonstrate their learning in a more appropriate context for some standards. For example, if students are expected to develop persuasive writing, a multiple-choice test cannot appropriately assess this skill. If the goal of a technology class is for students to create technology products, again, multiple-choice assessments or essays would not align to the learning target. Another benefit of authentic tasks is that they can access the highest level on Bloom's taxonomy, the Create level. As students brainstorm solutions (Planning), design a plan of action (Planning), and implement their plan (Producing), they are working at the highest cognitive levels. Selected-response questions cannot assess thinking on the Create level.

When designing an authentic task, teachers should first identify a role that is related to the intended learning target. Then, they need to identify the task, the product the students would produce, and the audience who would be interested in the product (see Figure 4.1).

Below are examples of authentic tasks in science, social studies, language arts, and math.

- ◆ **Science:** Acting as water conservationists (role), investigate ways to reduce water consumption in our school and propose an inexpensive and effective way to do so (task) in a presentation (product) to the principal (audience).

- ◆ **Social studies:** Acting as legislators, write a class constitution that identifies student rights, responsibilities, and duties as well as how the power will be distributed. This document will be used throughout the year to govern the classroom.

- ◆ **Language arts:** As an employee of a publishing company, select one book that was published fifty or more years ago by your company but is not widely known and would be appealing to the young adult market today. Prepare a persuasive presentation to convince the president of the publishing company to select your book for a new advertising campaign.

- ◆ **Math:** You have been hired as a Women's National Basketball Association recruiter. Review the statistics on six prospects for this year's draft and select one basketball player that you would recruit. Based on statistics alone, prepare a persuasive report to convince your boss that this player is the best recruit for your team. (This example could be changed to other sports depending on students' interests.)

Figure 4.1   **Designing an Authentic Task**

1. **Real-world role:** What job will the students be simulating?

2. **Task:** What is the task that the students will complete?

3. **Product:** What type of product will students construct? Could students create different products, allowing for student choice?

4. **Audience:** Who will view the product? Is there someone beyond the classroom that would be interested in this work?

Higher-Level Thinking

Scenarios, real-world examples, and authentic tasks all provide an opportunity for students to think at higher levels, assuming that the task or assessment is different from those they have previously encountered. There are many ways to infuse scenarios, real-world examples, and authentic tasks with critical thinking. One way is to include both relevant and irrelevant information in the task, thus requiring students to first identify the salient information before completing the task. For example, for the Apple marketing question mentioned previously, students might need to do research prior to answering the question. During the research process, students would need to identify information pertinent to answering the question.

Another way to assess student thinking is by asking students to identify examples of concepts in scenarios or real-world examples. In a social studies assessment about the way a coach leads a team, students could identify, based on the details in the scenario, what type of government (e.g., democracy, dictatorship, oligarchy) the coach most clearly represented. In science, an assessment could describe a girl drinking a cold beverage on a hot day and noticing the water beads on the outside of the glass. Students then must identify which concept is represented by the water beads (condensation).

Scenarios, real-world examples, and authentic tasks can also include complex situations requiring problem-solving. First, students must understand the situation by diagnosing and interpreting the nature and root causes of the problem. Students can identify possible solutions and evaluate each. Finally, students would develop and implement a plan.

Often in scenarios and real-world examples common misconceptions will be included, challenging students to identify the mistake. In math and science this is often termed "error analysis." After identifying the error, students can correct the mistake. In scenarios and real-world situations, students could also identify assumptions made in the situation and propose alternative interpretations.

While problem-solving is often used in math, other content areas can include problem-solving tasks with real dilemmas students must address. For example, a local gym has been unable to increase its membership. Students should determine the best way advertising can be used to increase the gym's membership. This would be an example of an authentic task as students determine a solution to a problem.

Another way to engage students in higher-level thinking is through decision-making tasks. Through decision-making, students evaluate alternatives by using developed criteria and then select the best course of action. For example, students can examine a country's postwar statistics and determine the country's next best foreign policy action. This exercise requires students to evaluate complex information and consider the economic, social, environmental, and/or religious ramifications of their decision. Often in decision-making, complex issues must be examined along with divergent points of view.

Design Tips

When utilizing scenarios or real-world examples for instructional tasks or assessments, teachers should consider the following items:

◆ Select the standard first. Always start by identifying the learning target or standard that will be the focus for your instructional task or assessment.

◆ Consider including relevant and irrelevant information so students learn to review information critically and select information appropriate to the task.

- Whenever possible, relate the scenarios, examples, or tasks to students' interests.

- Make sure the task matches the skill level of the students.

- Be sure the scenario does not provide trigger words that give away the answer. For example, if the question is about a concept and includes some of the typical words in the definition, they can cause students to automatically select the correct answer without thinking deeply.

- Decide on the assessment format. Scenarios and real-world examples could be structured in a multiple-choice or open-ended format. The end product of an authentic assessment could be in a variety of formats, including a presentation, a web page, or a piece of writing.

In Figure 4.2, steps for designing these types of items are enumerated.

Figure 4.2 **Steps to Design**

1. Identify the learning target or standard.
2. Search for real-world examples, create your own scenario, or design the authentic task.
3. Check the task or assessment to ensure it requires higher-level thinking processes.
   - Verify that the question requires students to understand introductory materials before answering the question.
   - Check to ensure that the scenario is new to the students.
   - Confirm that the answer is not directly in the introductory materials and that students must make connections to prior knowledge taught in the class. If the assessment is measuring students' conceptual understanding, be careful not to use terms that would make students automatically connect the question to an answer.
4. Determine if the assessment item is appropriate for the students' knowledge and skill level.
5. Ensure that the task or assessment contains all the information needed to answer the item unless students are expected to conduct research to complete the task.
6. Verify that the task or assessment item is clear, concise, and focused on the learning target.
7. Define the criteria that will be used to evaluate students' responses. If the question is open-ended, a scoring guide is needed.

Scenarios and Real-World Applications: Tasks and Assessment Examples

This section provides examples of instructional tasks and assessment examples of scenarios, real-world situations, and authentic tasks for math, science, social studies, and language arts. These examples will hopefully spur your creativity to design your own instructional tasks or assessments using these types of interpretive materials.

In the multiple-choice questions below, the correct answers are in bold type.

Math Examples

Scenarios

Example 1:

Cheyenne had six pencils when she walked into class today. Both Julie and Dari forgot to bring pencils. If Cheyenne shares her pencils with Julie and Dari, how many should each person get so everyone has an equal number?

a. 3   c. 1

b. 2   d. 6

Example 2:

Mr. Tevon is delivering a package. The instructions say, "My mailbox should be the third one down from the left." Circle the mailbox where Mr. Tevon should deliver the package.

Example 3:

Alfonso calculated 154 as the answer to the following expression: 34+10+100+10.

◆ Is Alfonso correct? Explain your answer using addition strategies to confirm his answer.

_____

_____

_____

Example 4:

Is Rafel late for school?

◆ If the current time is 7:10 a.m. and school starts at 7:45 a.m., how long does Rafel have to get to school?

_____

_____

◆ If he needs 20 minutes to get dressed and it takes 25 minutes to get to school, did he oversleep? If so, by how many minutes?

_____

_____

Real-World Examples

Example 1:

Who's the tallest in our class?

A. Complete the chart by recording the names of all group members and measuring their height in inches.

B. Rank your group members based on their height. A "1" ranking would mean a person was the tallest in your group.

C. Now, get together with another group and combine your data. Who is now the tallest? What is the average height of each group? Of the two groups combined? What happened to your numbers when you worked with the second group? Why?

Group Member's Name	Height in Inches	Ranking

Example 2:

Become a data analyzer!

A. Look online for a collection of data. It could be the height of trees, the length of rivers, the sales records of each iPhone, etc.

B. Using no more than the first twenty pieces of data, calculate the mean, median, mode, and range of the data collected.

C. State three conclusions you could draw from the data.

D. Post your data set and findings on the class blog. Be sure to label the measures of central tendency and the website where you found your data.

Example 3:

An iPod package has dimensions 4cm x 9cm x 14cm. An iPad package has dimensions 4cm x 19cm x 25cm.

◆ If the company uses rectangular boxes with 28cm x 76cm x 25cm dimensions, what is the maximum number of iPods that can fit in a box? _____

◆ What is the maximum number of iPads that can fit in the 28cm x 76cm x 25cm box? _____

Authentic Tasks

Example 1:

You have been hired by ESPN to profile one sports team that had an exceptional season this year.

A. Identify the sport and team you'd like to showcase.

B. Prepare a Prezi presentation (prezi.com) showing five statistics that demonstrate your team has had an exceptional season.

C. Share your presentation with the class and explain how those statistics were computed.

Example 2:

You are an architect building an apartment.

A. Use Floor Planner (www.floorplanner.com) to design an apartment.

B. Hardwood flooring costs $3 per square foot and carpeting costs $5 per square yard. Based on your design, which would be cheaper for your apartment? Show your work to justify your answer.

Example 3:

We are going to have a car race. As engineers, your group must figure out the best way to make your car go the farthest. You may use a ramp to launch your car. The car that goes the farthest will be the winner.

A. Build and test several ramps to determine the best design.

B. Create a bar graph to show how far your car went with each ramp (nces.ed.gov/nceskids/createagraph/).

C. Prepare your ramp for the competition!

D. Explain to the class why this ramp is the best design.

_____

_____

_____

Science Examples

Scenarios

Example 1:

Your friend wants to get a baby bunny as a pet but doesn't know how to take care of a bunny. Circle all the pictures that show basic needs of a bunny.

Example 2:

While watching your father cook supper, you saw that he left his metal spoon in the pan for several minutes. When he picked up the spoon to stir the food, the spoon was hot and burned his hand. He yelled and threw the metal spoon in the sink. Why might the spoon have burned him?

a. He is allergic to spoons.

b. It was too cold.

c. The spoon is metal.

d. The spoon couldn't have burned him.

Example 3:

Chantel wants to dye her hair blue for the upcoming ball game. She thinks the color will just wash out, even though the box says it is permanent. While the dye is in her hair, she feels her hair through the shower cap and it feels warm. What type of change is occurring in Chantel's hair?

a. environmental change

b. physical change

c. chemical change

d. material change

Real-World Examples

Example 1:

Science is everywhere in the world!

A. Choose a discipline of science that you find interesting (e.g., chemistry, biology, earth space science, physics)

B. Using the magazines provided, find seven real-world examples of your chosen scientific discipline. Cut them out and glue them to your paper.

C. In your groups, take turns sharing how each picture is a real-world example of your science discipline.

Example 2:

Science is important to everyone!

A. Research and create a video, Prezi (prezi.com) or Voki (www.voki.com), that introduces a person who made a significant contribution to science that is interesting to you.

B. In your presentation, mention at least three ways you are similar to the scientist (e.g., similar hometown, common interests, ethnicity, gender).

C. Persuade the class that this scientist is very important by highlighting three of his or her main accomplishments.

Example 3:

Adaptations are necessary for survival. Some animals change their appearance to adapt to a certain condition or environment. Others change their physiological condition or behavior in order to survive. How do you adapt to certain situations or environments?

A. Make a list of five physical adaptations and five behavioral adaptations you have made to survive.

_____

_____

_____

B. Share with the group your list and identify similarities among your lists.

Example 4:

My grandson was helping me in the garden. He pulled a weed out of the dirt and said, "Look at those stringy things hanging off the bottom of the weed." What part of the plant did he notice?

a. leaves

b. roots

c. flowers

d. stems

Authentic Tasks

Example 1:

We have been talking about the basic needs of animals.

A. Select a pet you would like to own. _____

B. Write a persuasive letter to your parents telling them how you will provide for the pet's basic needs of water, food, and shelter.

Example 2:

There are many examples of pollution in our community.

A. Identify a way we pollute in our community that affects the water cycle.

B. Create a public service announcement that will be aired on our school television show persuading viewers not to pollute in this way.

SCIENCE

Example 3:

We have been learning about acid rain. Do you think the rain that we get here is acidic?

A. In your lab notebook, make a hypothesis about the level of acidity in our rain.

B. In your group, test the pH of the rain that we have collected from our most recent rainfall. Do five trials of the pH to get an average.

C. As a scientist, create a report about your findings and include possible consequences to the environment and to people based on your findings.

Example 4:

Sally was driving to school this morning when she was in a car accident. Below you can see Sally's car. The driver of the other vehicle fled the scene immediately after the collision. Luckily Sally was not hurt. In her statement to the police, she said, "It was all a blur—I don't know if he hit me or I hit him." Police are trying to determine how this accident happened and how to best look for the other car involved in the accident.

As crime scene investigators, analyze the picture of Sally's car below and create a report for the police with the following elements:

◆ Determine what forces may have acted on Sally's car to cause the damage.

◆ Based on the evidence, hypothesize how the crash occurred (e.g., from which direction the other vehicle was coming, at which point the vehicles hit).

◆ Give the police details about the other vehicle that will help their search (e.g., where might the other vehicle have damage, would the other vehicle be similar in mass to Sally's car or not).

Social Studies Examples

Scenarios

Example 1:

Mayor Suzy wants to build a city park with a play area for children. The city park will have swings, slides, and monkey bars. How will the city pay for the park?

a. By collecting money from taxes

b. By borrowing money from the mayor

c. By giving money to the bank

d. By asking for money from another city

Example 2:

The teacher asked the students to identify the duties of the U.S. judicial branch. Kathy told the teacher that the judicial branch is responsible for making the laws. Is Kathy correct?

a. Yes, it is a correct statement.

b. No, the judicial branch enforces the laws.

c. No, making the laws is the purpose of the legislative branch.

Example 3:

Mark is having trouble deciding whether not eating food in the classroom is a rule or a law. With your group members discuss these questions.

◆ Is "not eating food in the classroom" a rule or a law?

◆ How do you know?

_____

_____

_____

_____

_____

_____

_____

_____

Example 4:

On the following list, place a check next to the examples of good citizenship. Cross out the poor citizenship examples and correct the bad examples on the lines provided below.

1. ____ A driver stops when she sees the stop sign.

2. ____ A person writes bad words on the store wall.

3. ____ A person takes out the trash for his elderly neighbor.

4. ____ A person volunteers at the local soup kitchen in the community.

5. ____ A person steals candy from the grocery store.

Corrected examples:

_____

_____

_____

_____

_____

Real-World Examples

Example 1:

If our classroom could be considered a type of government, which type would it be? Give two examples to support your answer.

_____

_____

_____

_____

_____

_____

Example 2:

Yesterday in class we worked on an art project with partners. Jerone wanted to paint the picture of the dog red, but Parker wanted to paint the dog yellow. What is the best way for Jerone and Parker to solve this problem?

  a. compromise   b. fight   c. compete

Example 3:

What is a want? What is a need?

A. Look at the magazine pictures on your table.

B. Select five pictures that are things you need. Glue them to your paper.

C. Select five pictures that are things you want. Glue them to the other side of your paper.

D. In your table group, take turns sharing why you classified each item as a want or a need.

Example 4:

With tight economic times, our school has to spend money wisely. Which of the following would be a "need" that must be provided by our school and cannot be eliminated in budget cuts?

a. Providing school lunches for those that didn't bring their lunch

b. Buying more computers

c. Purchasing additional physical education equipment

d. Repainting the restrooms to match the school colors

Authentic Tasks

Example 1:

We have discussed ways to solve conflict. Now it is your turn to propose a solution to a school problem.

1. In groups of four, choose one of the three school concerns that we brainstormed in class yesterday.
   - Improving school lunches
   - Adding more time for physical activity at school
   - Increasing the number of field trips

2. Research the issue and determine the best way our school can address the concern.

3. Create a Prezi presentation (prezi.com). In your Prezi please include:
   - Description of the school problem
   - How you arrived at your solution
   - Your solution

4. Share your presentation. The principal will select the best problem-solution presentation and consider ways to implement the solution.

Let's make a deal! Today you brought two inexpensive items you would like to trade and sell.

1. Select one of the items you brought today. Visit with other sellers and try to trade for something better. Both sellers must agree to switch items in order for the trade to be complete.

2. After the conclusion of the bartering time, record your thoughts on these questions.

    ◆ What difficulties did you face while trying to make a deal?

    ◆ When have you bartered for an item?

3. Get your second item. You now have $10 in class money and your item. Visit with other sellers and use your cash to purchase items. Both the seller and the buyer must agree on the price.

4. After finishing the class money activity, record your thoughts on these questions.

    ◆ How did having cash make selling and buying easier?

    ◆ Do you prefer to barter or use cash when purchasing items? Give at least three reasons to support your opinion.

5. Create a Voki (www.voki.com) to present to the class that summarizes your answers to the questions above.

Example 3:

At the beginning of the school year, we will collaboratively develop rules for our class.

1. In your teams of four, decide on five classroom rules. Consider the bulleted points below when designing your rules.

    ◆ How should I treat other students in the classroom?

    ◆ What I am responsible for in the classroom?

    ◆ How should I treat my teacher in the classroom?

2. Use Glogster (www.edu.glogster.com) to design a poster displaying your proposed rules. Be prepared to persuade your classmates with reasons why your rules will best help create a learning community in our classroom.

3. In front of the class, groups will display posters and justify why each rule is important.

4. Finally, the class will vote to select which rules will be used in our class.

Language Arts Examples

Scenarios

Example 1:

This morning, you rode the bus from your house to school. Your parents drove the car to work in the opposite direction from your school. You talked to your best friend while riding the bus to pass the time. Why did you ride the bus?

  a. To talk to your friend

  b. To get from your house to school

  c. To do your homework

  d. To sleep

Example 2:

Circle the first word of this sentence.

◆ Today at recess David threw a ball at Tamara.

Example 3:

Last week we had a spelling bee. Draw what you remember from the spelling bee. Write one sentence about what happened.

Real-World Examples

Example 1:

In the story we read, *A Porcupine Named Fluffy*, Fluffy the Porcupine has needles that give him trouble. Draw a picture about a time that you had a problem.

Example 2:

Characters in books are often very similar to the people we know in our own lives.

  A. Pick a character from *Perloo the Bold* and explain two ways you are similar to the character.

  B. Describe one way the character is different from you.

  C. Would you be friends with the character if they attended our school? Why or why not?

Example 3:

Reread pages 2 and 3 from *The Trouble with May Amelia* and discuss the following questions with your partner:

◆ Identify three clues in the text that show how May Amelia feels about being a girl.

◆ What are two feelings that you and May Amelia have in common?

After your discussion in pairs, I will group two pairs together to make a group of four to share and compare your ideas.

Authentic Tasks

Example 1:

In "Nice New Neighbors," the mice act out a play and make new friends.

A. With your group, write down a sentence telling one way you could make a new friend at school.

B. Decide how you could act out your idea.

C. Our class will present our ideas at our school's next morning meeting. One group member will say the sentence while the other group members act it out.

Example 2:

In *Charlotte's Web*, Wilbur is saved from being eaten because Charlotte creates messages in her webs about him. At our school fewer students are reading books this year than five years ago. How can we create a message to save reading?

A. As a group, discuss the possible ways you could fix this problem. Research ways other schools have addressed the problem.

B. Select the best solution and determine a plan to promote reading in our school.

C. Create a presentation to deliver to the librarian and principal outlining your plan. Use Slide Rocket (www.sliderocket.com) to design your presentation.

Example 3:

Pick something that you do well. It should be something that you can explain to other people.

◆ Write a "how-to" piece that has step-by-step guidelines.

Discuss

◆ Where have you previously observed scenarios, real-world examples, and authentic tasks being used as instructional tools or assessments?

◆ How are teachers in your building using scenarios, real-world examples, and authentic tasks?

◆ In your classroom, how could you use scenarios, real-world examples, and authentic tasks?

Take Action

◆ Design a scenario, real-world example, and authentic task that you could use as an instructional tool or assessment.

◆ Examine the instructional tasks and assessments you currently use. Where could you replace or include an instructional activity or assessment with a scenario, real-world example, and/or authentic task to improve the quality of instruction in your classroom?

5

Interpretive Exercises: Visual Materials

The human mind, once stretched to a new idea, never goes back to its original dimensions.

—Oliver Wendell Holmes

Visuals are another source of materials for creating interpretive exercises. Images abound in our culture, from television shows to billboards. In schools, visuals from media, books, and a variety of other sources are used in instruction to build student understandings.

There are several benefits to using visuals. One benefit is that visuals assist beginning readers, English language learners, and students with reading disabilities by helping them understand the task through pictures instead of text. Many students who have difficulty with reading can express their knowledge through pictures and learn especially well from visuals. In addition, many students prefer to learn in a visual way. I personally first examine the diagrams in a technical guide and then, if necessary, read the instructions. Research has found that people process visuals 60,000 faster than text (3M Corporation, 2001). Thus, visuals assist in speedier student comprehension.

This chapter will describe different types of visual materials and how to use them to create high-level thinking opportunities. Recommendations for designing tasks and assessments using visual materials are provided, followed by multiple examples from several content areas.

Types of Visuals

There are several types of visuals that can be used in instructional tasks and assessments: illustrations, charts, data tables, maps, and diagrams. In some instances, visual materials can be combined with scenarios to create a challenging task. For example, students could be given a scenario of a scientific experiment with a data chart of unexpected results. Students could draw conclusions on what potentially caused those results. This section will focus on the many ways illustrations, charts, data tables, maps, and diagrams can be used in instructional tasks and assessments.

Illustrations or Objects

Illustrations, including advertisements, paintings, pictures, and cartoons, often provide vivid and captivating images for students to explore. Traditionally illustrations have been used in content areas like art class when examining paintings or perhaps in English classes when examining advertisements for persuasive techniques. However, illustrations can be used in all content areas.

Advertisements are a rich source for images. Students can analyze advertisements to identify persuasion techniques and examine whether the claims are accurate. Students can investigate using their knowledge of math and science to confirm the claims. For example, does a new exercise product produce results? Students can also examine advertisements from a historical perspective to identify common assumptions held at an earlier time period or draw conclusions about the culture of that time.

There are also many paintings and pictures that can be used as visual materials. A painting could be examined for clues in identifying the historical time period for an English or social studies class. Students can examine the similarities and differences between the paintings and the writing styles of a certain time period. A painting could be used as a stimulus for students to generate a creative story about what is happening in the painting or picture. In math class, students can examine mathematical principles in art. For example, when are geometric figures aesthetically pleasing in art? How do artists use mathematic ideas of proportion in paintings? In science, students can examine how paintings and pictures reflect scientific ideas of the historical time period. A new rising source of visuals is infographics, which are visual representations of information, data, or knowledge. Students can examine infographics already created or design their own. A website called Visual.ly provides many infographics examples.

Cartoons are a way to inject humor and critical thinking into a class while providing another source of images. Students can examine cartoons to identify the cartoonist's point of view. Students can detect stereotypes, caricatures, and symbolism. Examining a cartoon with characters talking about how they answered a math problem, students could identify their mistake in reasoning. Teachers and students can draw their own cartoons or create them online using websites such as ToonDoo or Make Beliefs Comix. When students create their own cartoons, they can summarize information and profile their point of view on a topic.

In addition, a real object can be used as a visual. For example, students might analyze a fossil, old map, photograph, piece of art, or postcard to draw conclusions about how it was created, how old it is, and where it comes from. Students could become detectives trying to unearth clues about a mysterious object.

Charts and Data Tables

Another source of images is data tables and charts. Data tables organize numbers or information in a systematized fashion. Using this organized information, students can then create charts. Charts are graphical representations of data. There are numerous types of charts: line charts, pie charts, organizational charts, and flow charts. While charts are often used in math and science classes, many content areas can use charts and tables to organize information about population trends, public opinion, temperature, interest rates, stock market prices, scientific experiment results, and mathematical data.

Charts and data tables challenge students to cognitively process the information at high levels as they interpret data and draw conclusions. Charts and tables are often used to persuade audiences. Students must learn to scrutinize these, as data are not always represented accurately. Inaccurate representations of data can lead to faulty conclusions. Students can also be given a data table or chart with headings not completely identified. Students could then generate possible headings for the data table or chart.

Students can also collect information and create their own data tables and charts to depict the information in an illustrative form. In social studies, students could survey others to determine the key political issues affecting elementary students or which environmental solution would best address a local problem. In English class, students could create a data table or chart to support their persuasive argument.

Maps and Diagrams

Finally, maps and diagrams provide numerous images for students to evaluate. Maps are a representation of Earth's surface often showing direction, size, or distance. There are climate, economic, resource, physical, political, road, and topographical maps. In English, students can examine the geographical location of the setting of a novel and assess if and how the geography affected the plot development. In science and social studies classes, students can examine maps to determine how geography impacts settlement patterns.

A diagram offers a symbolic representation of information. Often diagrams are used to help readers visualize information. Diagrams can represent information on numerous topics, including the human body, plot development, and the technical structure of objects like a spacecraft. In addition, students can use many different types of graphic organizers, including cause-and-effect organizers, fishbone diagrams, Venn comparison diagrams, and concept maps. Students can create their own diagrams to build their conceptual understanding. They can also analyze various diagrams on the same topic, identifying similarities and differences between the representations while finding irregularities. Teachers can give students several diagrams to analyze and have the students select which diagram best represents the information.

Higher-Level Thinking

As with all interpretive exercises, since the introductory information provides new material for students to understand, minimally all tasks and assessments would be on the Understand level of Bloom's taxonomy. At the Understand level, students can interpret the meaning and draw conclusions from the visual materials. They can compare and contrast various visuals. When examining visuals, students can identify examples or non-examples of an identified concept. For instance, students could circle all the pictures that represent early Greek architecture. Students could create an example that would represent a given data set or chart. Also, students could classify visual materials in various categories and provide defensible reasons to justify their classifying system—for example, when investigating fossils, students could decide to group all the fossils that showed marine life in one category. Students can use visuals to make analogies or metaphors of concepts studied. For instance, how is a picture of a sculpture like a character in a book? Based on information from a data table or chart, students can also make predictions about what might happen in the future or how the data could impact other factors. For example, based on a chart of a country's deforestation trends, students could hypothesize how the economy and living conditions are currently being affected and will be impacted in the future if the trends continue.

Tasks on the Apply level of Bloom's taxonomy usually require students to use a skill. For example, students can use visual materials to create calculations, identify correct sentence diagrams, and determine longitude and latitude on maps. In addition, students could devise formulas to represent data sets.

Students can also engage in analysis and evaluation. When examining paintings, pictures, and cartoons, students can be challenged to identify possible biases or points of view. Students can also identify errors in visual materials. After reading, students could design their own graphic representation or diagram of the written material. To evaluate, students can select an image that best represents a historical time period and defend their choice. Students could select and explain which exercise plan depicted in a chart best meets the particular needs of a third-grade student.

At the Create level of Bloom's taxonomy, students can design visual materials to bolster their persuasive remarks, to support their scientific recommendations, or to express their viewpoint. This might involve students taking a survey and collecting data or designing their own political cartoon.

Design Tips

Some tips are provided below to assist you in designing interpretive materials using images.

◆ Find images on the Internet. There is a wealth of visuals available on the Internet. Due to the ease of searching the Internet, it is a quick way to access images. Most search engines provide an option to restrict the search to images only, producing numerous images for the teacher or student to select from for an instructional task or assessment. However, be aware of copyright protections on images.

◆ Use new images. As previously mentioned, to ensure higher-level thinking, use images that students have not already analyzed. If you use a familiar image, ensure that students are thinking about it in a new way.

◆ Make sure that the image is required to answer the assessment. Since the image will be in the introductory material, the assessment or task should require students to use the image in some way. If the students can answer the question without looking at the graphic, then the image is unnecessary.

◆ Use a clear image. Whether the image is found online or copied from a book, make sure the graphic is clear, particularly if it will be reproduced. When images are copied or scaled to differing sizes or when color graphics are printed in black and white, they may become distorted, reducing the clarity of the visuals. Visuals need to be large enough for students to appropriately interpret them. Some teachers include small, black-and-white visuals on an assessment, but also use a larger color version on the computer screen.

For steps to design assessments with visual materials, see Figure 5.1.

Figure 5.1 Steps to Design Assessments Using Visual Materials

1. Identify a learning target or standard.
2. Search online or in texts for visual materials that align to the learning target or standard.
3. Select printed materials that are new to the students.
4. Make sure visuals are clear.
5. Verify that the question requires students to understand the visual before answering the question.
6. Check to make sure that the assessment item is appropriate for students' knowledge and skill level.
7. Ensure that the assessment item is clear, concise, and focused on the learning target.
8. If it is an open-ended task or assessment, define the criteria that will be used to evaluate students' responses.

Visual Tasks and Assessment Examples

This section provides examples of instructional tasks and assessments using illustrations, objects, maps, diagrams, charts, and data tables for the math, science, social studies, and language arts content areas. By examining these examples, you can get ideas to design your own instructional tasks or assessments using these types of interpretive materials.

In the multiple-choice questions below, the correct answers are in bold type.

Math Examples

Illustrations or Objects

Example 1:

Martha and Janet have lollipops, gum drops, and candy canes in a bag as shown above. Martha said the fraction representing the number of lollipops and candy canes is 10/16. Janet disagreed and said 5/8.

A. Who is correct?

B. Explain how you arrived at your conclusion.

_____

_____

_____

_____

_____

Example 2:

Greg has bought four dogs and wants to keep them in an enclosed area. The picture shows a model of the fence. If the required area for four dogs is five square miles and each two centimeters on the picture model equals one mile, does Greg have a large enough area? If not, what would be the dimensions of a fence that would enclose exactly five square miles?

Example 3:

Design Shape People!

A. Using Microsoft Word or another drawing program, create a drawing of a person using at least four of the geometric shapes we have studied.

B. Post your work on the wall of our classroom.

C. Walk around and review the Shape People created by your classmates. Record the artists' names and circle all the shapes used in their drawings in the chart provided.

Student's Name	Shapes Used					
	Circle	Triangle	Square	Rectangle	Hexagon	Pentagon
	Circle	Triangle	Square	Rectangle	Hexagon	Pentagon

Example 4:

Symmetry is all around us.

◆ In this picture, how many lines of symmetry are represented? _____

◆ Do humans have the same number of symmetry lines? Why or why not?

_____

_____

_____

_____

Charts and Data Tables

Example 1:

Item	Quantity
Tents	3 total
Stakes	6 per tent
Poles	3 per tent
Ropes	7 total
Water	2 liters per person
Repellent	1 can per person

Six people are going on a campout. This table shows the equipment they will pack. Use the table to answer the following questions.

1. It takes nine minutes to put up one tent. How long will it take to set up all the tents?

    a. 3 minutes

    b. 27 minutes

    c. 18 minutes

    d. 6 minutes

2. If all the campers want the same amount of room in the tent, how many people will sleep in each tent?

    a. 3 campers

    b. 6 campers

    c. 1 camper

    d. 2 campers

3. How many poles are needed for all the tents?

    a. 9 poles

    b. 3 poles

    c. 6 poles

    d. 27 poles

Example 2:

Here is a list of the number of hits for each member of a softball team this season. Which conclusion can be drawn from the data set?

Player	Hits
Abby	10
Chantelle	25
Sari	21
Sarah	3
Violet	8
Zoey	7
Becky	3
Brie	1
Danielle	13
Latitia	27

a. Because the range is 26, it can be concluded that the team has varying levels of hitting skills.

b. Because Violet has 8 hits and is 5th on the list when you rank the players, it can be concluded that she'll also be the mean of the data set.

c. Because the mode of the data set is 3, it can be concluded that the team isn't very good.

d. Since the range of the data set is 26, it can be concluded that the team is a strong team.

Example 3:

Duran has $20.00 when he walks into his favorite store, Candy Craze. He sees the sign with the candy prices.

If he wants to spend all but $2 of his money, what is the greatest number of packages of candy he can buy?

Candy	Price
Lollipops	$1.50
1 lb of Jolly Ranchers	$3.00
8-pack of Hershey Bars	$1.75
Box of Nerds	$2.00
Bag of Reese Cups	$2.00
1 lb of M & M's	$2.50

a. 8

b. 10

c. **12**

d. 14

Example 4:

	CD	DVD	Blu-Ray	Nintendo DS	Nintendo 3DS
Height (in inches)	1/4	1/2	3/8	5/8	1/2
Width (in inches)	5	5 1/4	5 1/4	4 7/8	4 3/4
Length (in inches)	5 1/2	7 1/2	6 1/2	5 1/4	5 1/4

List the five products above in order from the smallest to largest volume.

Maps and Diagrams

Example 1:

Ms. Kim has ten book shelves. Some have books and others hold puzzles and games. A student in the class has drawn a diagram to show the books on the shelves. Which formula could be used to calculate the total number of books on the bookcase?

a. 10×8

b. 5×8

c. $10 + 8$

d. $8 + 8 + 8 + 8$

Example 2:

Using the scale provided, determine the distance between Doolittle and Dillon. Explain how you determined the answer.

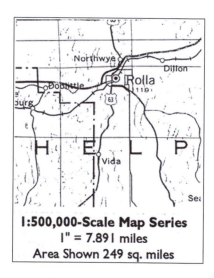

1:500,000-Scale Map Series
1" = 7.891 miles
Area Shown 249 sq. miles

Example 3:

Below is a picture of bowling balls. The weight of each ball is shown. If the ball are supposed to be in order from the lightest on the left to the heaviest on the right, mark which bowling ball is not in the correct order.

Science Examples

Illustrations or Objects

Example 1:

Look at the objects I have provided you and classify them as paper, wood, or metal. After examining the object, circle the category below.

Paper clip	Paper	Wood	Metal
Twig	Paper	Wood	Metal
Pencil	Paper	Wood	Metal
Newspaper	Paper	Wood	Metal
Magnet	Paper	Wood	Metal
Magazine	Paper	Wood	Metal

Example 2:

Examine the three Styrofoam cups of bean plants.

A. Identify which plant represents each part of the plant life cycle: life, growth and development, reproduction or death.

B. After classifying the plants, draw a picture of the plant that represents each category in the chart below.

Life	Growth and Development	Reproduction or Death

Example 3:

After watching the "Gummy Bear Experiment" with molten potassium chlorate performed by your teacher, answer the following questions.

A. Was the "Gummy Bear Experiment" an example of a physical or a chemical change? _____

B. Explain your answer with 2 reasons or observations.

_____

_____

_____

_____

_____

Example 4:

Examine the pictures below. Propose at least one reason why the plants could have grown in this particular way. Incorporate your understanding of adaptation in your answer.

Plant A

Plant B

_____

_____

_____

_____

_____

Example 5:

Based on the picture above, which body system would be most impacted by the hit?

a. nervous system

b. circulatory system

c. immune system

d. endocrine system

Charts and Data Tables

Example 1:

Item	Length of Ramp	Time
Toy car	3 feet	20 seconds
Toy truck	3 feet	10 seconds
Toy eighteen-wheeler	3 feet	7 seconds

1. Based on the table above, which toy went at the fastest speed?

   a. car

   b. truck

   c. **eighteen-wheeler**

   d. They all went at the same speed.

2. Based on the data table, draw a conclusion as to why the toy in the previous question went the fastest.

   a. The slowest toy could have been on carpeted ramp instead of a wooden ramp.

   b. The fastest toy is heavier than the other two toys.

   c. The fastest toy could have been pushed, while the slow toys coasted down the ramp.

   d. **All of the above are reasonable conclusions.**

Example 2:

Cut out the pictures below and glue them into the appropriate category on the chart.

Solid	Liquid	Gas

Example 3:

Complete the data table by calculating speed; then use the data table to answer the following questions.

Object and Surface	Distance	Time	Speed (d/t)
Ball on shag rug	5 feet	5 seconds	
Ball on tile floor	15 feet	3 seconds	
Ball on carpet	10 feet	4 seconds	
Ball on ice	20 feet	3 seconds	

1. Which ball had the greatest speed?

   a. Ball on shag rug

   b. Ball on tile floor

   c. Ball on carpet

   d. Ball on ice

2. Which ball had the least speed?

   a. Ball on shag rug

   b. Ball on tile floor

   c. Ball on carpet

   d. Ball on ice

3. Explain why the speed of the ball was affected by different surfaces.

_____

_____

_____

_____

Maps and Diagrams

Example 1:

What does this picture show?

   a. magnets attracted to each other

   b. magnets repelling each other

   c. horseshoes stuck together

   d. magnets that have lost their dipoles

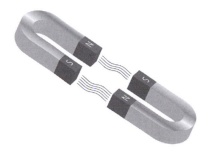

Example 2:

Look at the figure below and examine the anatomies of the person and animals.

A. Describe two things in common about the anatomies of all four animals.

_____

_____

_____

_____

_____

_____

_____

B. Explain one difference between the anatomies of the person and one of the animals.

_____

_____

_____

_____

_____

_____

_____

Example 3:

Examine the diagram of the layers of Earth.

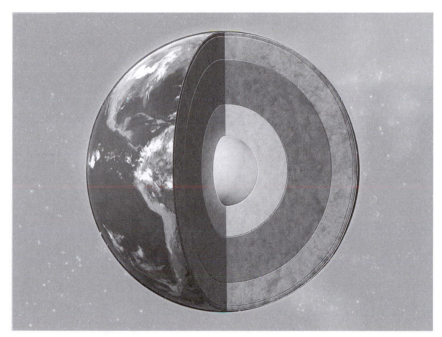

A. Label the layers of Earth on the diagram.

B. Create a metaphor by comparing the layers of Earth to another object.

_____

_____

_____

_____

_____

_____

_____

_____

_____

_____

_____

_____

_____

_____

_____

Social Studies Examples

Illustrations or Objects

Example 1:

What does this picture show people following?

Circle the correct answer:

Rules   Laws

Example 2:

Examine the picture of Zulu tribe members from South Africa.

A. Describe two ways the people in the image express their culture.

_____

_____

_____

_____

B. One man is holding a shield. Why might the shield be important to his culture?

_____

_____

_____

_____

C. What is one way your life might be different from theirs?

_____

_____

_____

_____

D. What is one way your life is similar to the way they live?

_____

_____

_____

_____

Example 3:

How much do you know about advertising? Your advertising skills will help you be successful on this assignment.

1. In your small group, decide what item you would like to sell.

2. Read the text provided describing the basics for advertising. Feel free to explore other advertising web links to prepare for the next step.

3. Using Kerpoof (www.kerpoof.com), brainstorm and then design your advertisement, making sure to describe your product and the price as well as following the best advertising techniques.

4. After completing your advertisement, in your group analyze the advertisements of the other groups of students and answer the following questions:

   ◆ What product or service is being advertised?

   ◆ What advertising techniques did they use?

   ◆ Do you think the price is reasonable? Explain.

   ◆ What are two ways they could improve their advertisement?

Example 4:

Based on this image of the James-town colony, what was the main concern when building the colony?

a. security

b. food supply

c. diseases

d. natural materials

Example 5:

The photo is a picture of Venice, Italy. Water is an important geographic feature of the city.

◆ Describe two ways shown in the picture that the people of Venice adapted to this natural feature.

_____

_____

_____

Charts and Data Tables

Example 1:

In groups of three, visit the four stations to record the names of four lemonade stores. Then, count how many lemonade boxes are left at each store and record that number in the "Unsold Boxes" column. As a group, figure out how many boxes of lemonade each store sold. Record this information in your chart. Answer the following questions:

◆ Which store had the highest demand for lemonade?

◆ Which store had the lowest demand for lemonade?

◆ What could the store with the lowest demand do to increase lemonade sales?

Name of Shop	Supply	Unsold Boxes	Sold
	10		
	10		
	10		
	10		

Example 2:

Review the following profit chart. The last column asks if the owner should continue or discontinue selling the product. If you think the owner should keep selling the product, write "yes." If you don't support the owner continuing to sell the product, write "no."

Business	Product	Profit in 2011	Profit in 2012	Yes or No
Cathy's Chocolate Store	Fudge	$200	$400	
Larry's Lighting Store	Lights	$80	$30	
Barry's Baseball Store	Baseballs	$100	$250	
Pat's Pet Store	Puppies	$500	$400	

◆ After viewing the chart, choose one of the stores you decided should keep producing its product and explain your reasoning.

_____

_____

◆ After viewing the chart, chose one of the stores you decided should not keep producing its product and explain your reasoning.

_____

_____

Example 3:

Cut out the following pictures. Paste them in the appropriate column on the chart.

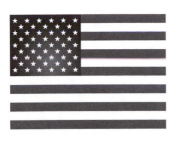

United States Symbols	United States Landmarks	United States Holidays

Example 4:

Examine the chart and answer the questions below.

City	Average Temperature in January (°F)	Average Temperature in July (°F)
Seattle, WA	47	76
Chicago, IL	31	84
Honolulu, HI	81	88

Source: www.weather.com

◆ Which city do you think has the highest average temperature?

_____

◆ Which city probably has four strongly different seasons?

_____

◆ Explain two ways these weather patterns would impact the way of life in **each** city.

_____

_____

Maps and Diagrams

Example 1:

Based on your understanding of climates and the physical features in America, use the map to respond to the following questions:

1. What cities could you visit in the United States if you wanted to collect sea shells? Explain your answer.

_____

_____

_____

_____

2. What cities in the United States would you visit if you wanted to go skiing? Explain your answer, making connections to your knowledge of climate regions.

_____

_____

_____

3. What cities in the United States would you visit if you wanted to see a cactus? Explain your answer, making connections to your knowledge of climate regions.

_____

_____

_____

4. What cities in the United States would you visit if you wanted to see a farm? Explain your answer, making connections to your knowledge of the physical features in America.

_____

_____

_____

Example 2:

In this unit we will be studying explorers.

1. Choose a famous French, English, or Spanish explorer in American history.

2. Research the explorer and the impact the explorer had on American history. Include the following:

   ◆ Why is the explorer famous?

   ◆ Why might some people view the explorer negatively?

   ◆ Without this explorer, how might your life or community be different?

3. Create a mind map organizing your thoughts about the above questions using Mindmeister (www.mindmeister.com) or Bubbl.us (bubbl.us). Be prepared to present your mind map to the class.

Example 3:

I drew my mental map showing how I get from the grocery store to my house. We also played a game with you raising "Yes" or "No" cards based on if you thought my statements about my mental map were correct or incorrect. Now we are going to walk around the school for you to observe things you'd like to put on your mental map of the things around the school.

◆ During our walk, draw pictures in your notebook of the things you'd like to remember to put on your map.

◆ On your mental map, you should include at least three landforms (e.g., tree or bush) and our school building.

Language Arts Examples

Illustrations or Objects

Example 1:

We just read *When I Grow Up* and we learned about community helpers. Circle the community helper who can put out a fire.

Example 2:

In *A Series of Unfortunate Events: The Reptile Room*, Uncle Monty has a room with snakes in it.

A. Do you think the children like or dislike the room? Why?

_____

_____

B. How do you think the pictures to the right show how people can view snakes differently?

_____

_____

_____

Example 3:

We read *Are You My Mother?* by P. D. Eastman. **Circle** the picture that shows another mother.

Charts and Data Tables

Example 1:

Based on your understanding of *On the Wings of Heroes*, create a comparison chart that shows three similarities and three differences between Davy Bowman's father and his brother. Use the ReadWriteThink website to write your comparison (www.readwritethink.org/files/resources/interactives/venn/).

Example 2:

In *James and the Giant Peach*, James has a wild adventure. Which one of these decisions was **NOT** made by the character beside it? Mark out the character that is incorrectly matched with the decision.

Character	Decision
Centipede	Bites the stem of the peach so it rolls away
Spider	Acts as bait to attract the seagulls
Old Man	Gives James crocodile tongues
Spike and Sponge	Mistreat James after his parents die

Example 3:

In *Amber Brown Is Not a Crayon*, Amber is sad because Justin is going to live in another city. Circle the group of people on the chart who would probably best understand how Amber Brown feels.

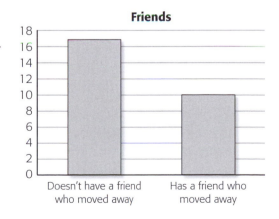

LANGUAGE ARTS

Maps and Diagrams

Example 1:

In *I Am the Ice Worm*, Allison is in a plane crash. Compare the precipitation of Allison's home in Southern California to the precipitation of Alaska, where her plane crashes. How different is the climate in the two regions? (1 inch = 25.4mm)

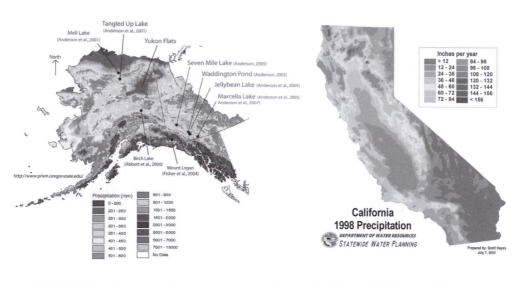

_____

_____

_____

Example 2:

After reading *A Pirate's Guide to First Grade*, circle the item that the main character in the book would probably want.

Example 3:

In *Math Curse*, the main character starts to see everything as a math problem. Complete the chart below, noting her strengths and weaknesses as she struggles to use math in everyday situations.

Strengths	Weaknesses

Discuss

◆ Where have you previously observed visual materials embedded into instructional tasks or assessments?

◆ How are teachers in your building using visual materials?

◆ In your classroom, how could you use visual materials?

Take Action

◆ Design an instructional task or assessment using an illustration, object, data table, chart, map, or diagram.

◆ Examine the instructional tasks and assessments you currently use. Where could you replace an instructional task or assessment with one that includes visual materials to improve the quality of your instruction?

6

Interpretive Exercises: Quotations

In thinking critically, we take command of the meanings we create.
—Richard Paul and Linda Elder

A third way to increase the level of cognitive complexity in instructional tasks and assessments is by using quotations. Teachers can use short quotes, a few sentences long, or longer passages from written sources. Additionally, media can provide quotes through news and television shows, movies, and songs. Short quotes, passages, and media clips are useful ways to provide introductory materials in an interpretive exercise in order to infuse critical thinking into classroom tasks and assessments.

Many of the questions on standardized tests and materials in college courses include quotes, interpretive readings, and media clips, with students expected to make thoughtful inferences and determine perspectives. This expectation goes beyond the traditional worksheets and textbook end-of-the-section questions that require students to find the correct answers without deeply processing the reading. Through understanding and analyzing quotes, students build stronger conceptual understandings and thinking skills.

This chapter will profile different types of quotes and show how they can be embedded into instructional experiences to create high-level thinking opportunities. Recommendations for designing tasks and assessments using quotes are provided, followed by multiple examples from several content areas.

Types of Quotations

Short Quotes

Short quotes are a few sentences in length. A quote from a student or a famous person can provide an immediate way to initiate a lesson, become a classroom activity, or be used as an assessment. Quotes can be used in all subject areas. For instance, Shaquille O'Neal, a famous basketball player, said, "I'm tired of hearing about money, money, money, money, money. I just want to play the game, drink Pepsi, wear Reebok." This quote could easily relate to content in several subjects.

- ◆ Social studies: What person in history could be characterized by this quote?

- ◆ Language arts: What characters in a text would probably agree with this quote?

Passages

Longer reading passages from primary sources, literature, and informational sources (e.g., journals, web pages, newspapers, magazine articles) can also be used. Under the Common Core State Standards, teachers of all subjects are expected to teach literacy. Thus, it is appropriate that all subject areas incorporate reading excerpts and passages into classroom instruction.

Primary sources provide firsthand testimony from someone who lived during a certain time period. Primary sources can be used in social studies classes to examine feelings and viewpoints during a particular era. Language arts teachers can use primary sources as a main text or to build prior knowledge before the class reads another text from the same time period. Science teachers can use primary sources to showcase scientific perspectives during certain eras in history. Students can also examine the writer's point of view and assumptions, while looking for inaccurate statements in the writing.

Teachers can integrate a variety of forms of literature, including novels, poems, dramas, and short stories. If the texts are lengthy, classes could examine an excerpt from the work. Most students love stories and poems that relate to students' interests. For instance, students can determine if a poem titled "Hypotenuse," written by Eric Rose, or, as he likes to be called, "Mr. R.," on his Math Story website correctly describes the hypotenuse. Students could even write their own original poem on the topic.

There is also an abundance of informational sources in texts and online for teachers to use as supplementary materials for passages. For example, students could read passages from *Bloodletting Instruments in the National Museum of History and Technology* by Audrey Davis. In a social studies class, students could examine the impact of the practice of bloodletting on the culture and how this medical procedure emerged and waned. In science class, students can examine the impact of this practice on patients' health.

To prepare for the academic writing expected in college, students can critique other student-written research papers to help them become better writers themselves. In addition, web pages, newspaper articles, and magazines showcase current perspectives and information that can connect to concepts being studied. Since selecting quality sources is an important skill, students can examine informational sources to assess their accuracy. There are several websites that are "fake" or "spoofs." For example, a site titled Dihydrogen Monoxide—DHMO Homepage claims that dihydrogen monoxide, otherwise known as water, is dangerous, which it is not. With the plethora of informational sources, students need to practice identifying quality sources of information.

Media Clips

A third source of engaging quotes is media clips. Online media, movie and television clips, songs, and your own footage provide many sources of media clips. Students often enjoy these instructional tasks and assessments because they are visually interesting and include sound and/or music and sometimes drama. For teachers, the Internet provides a multitude of free media clips. A recent Internet search for a video on states of matter produced 57 million video options. In addition, many search engines will alert you if new videos are posted on an identified topic. The ease of acquiring media clips allows you to integrate this resource effortlessly into classroom instruction.

Using media clips from online is a great way of making real-world connections to your content. YouTube, CNN, local news stations, and a variety of companies produce online media daily that can be connected to what is being learned in the class. English classes can examine how current news applies to themes in literature. In science, students can examine news reports about new drugs and science inventions that apply to concepts studied. In math and science classes, students can examine how media use math and science to inform and persuade the public.

Movie and television clips are another interesting way to make connections between the lesson content and popular movies and television shows. For example, how are the governments in *The Hunger Games*, *Star Wars*, and America similar and different?

Song lyrics often show the feelings of people. Using lyrics in class is a way to analyze perspectives and assumptions. It also appeals to students and their interest in music. In social studies and language arts classes, students can examine song lyrics to identify opinions during a historical period. In addition, students can make connections between current music lyrics and viewpoints of historical people, events, or novels. For example, students can make connections between a country music song and Thomas Jefferson's agrarian beliefs.

Many songs provide a way for students to learn basic concepts. "Why Does the Sun Shine?" is an example of a song and a video that teach the purpose of the sun. A recent search for songs about multiplication revealed 3,000 songs available online. With a proliferation of songs available, students can analyze songs to determine if they are accurate. Students can also create their own songs to demonstrate their understandings. Students can take a current tune and create their own lyrics for the music. In my class, students took the tune of "The Itsy Bitsy Spider" and wrote lyrics about the "Itsy Bitsy" Pilgrims. Students can also use software such as Garage Band to creatively design their own music or podcasts about content.

With smartphone applications and other technologies that can record video, students can make their own videos. At a recent baseball practice, I was asked to video a pitcher warming up. The pitcher wanted to use the video of him along with a later added narration to explain how Newton's laws of motion were involved in the pitching and catching. While the assignment only required him to identify one law of motion, the student became so interested in the project that he planned to explain how all three of Newton's laws were shown in the pitching and catching video.

Higher-Level Thinking

Quotes, passages, and media clips can provide ways to reach higher-level thinking. Since the quotes, passages, or clips are new to the students, the task or assignment would be at least on the Understand level of Bloom's taxonomy. At this level, one way to assess comprehension of the introductory materials is by asking students to summarize information or make inferences. Another option is to require students to mentally make connections between the introductory materials and background information. Additionally, students could be asked to identify or provide another example of a concept in a quote. Using two quotes, passages, or media clips, students could compare and contrast the informational sources. Furthermore, after reading the quote, students can select who might have authored the quote.

On the Analyze level of Bloom's taxonomy, passages and quotes often have sections that are irrelevant to the assessment. Students can practice eliminating information in the quotes that is not relevant to the task or identifying misconceptions mentioned. Students can also organize information from a passage or media clip in a diagram. Through their reading and listening to media sources, students can be challenged to identify biases, assumptions, intentions, or points of view. At the Evaluate level, tasks can engage students in the decision-making process by identifying criteria and ranking options. For example, students could select which informational source best represents the achievements of a famous author or leader. In science, students can select which media clip best explains the rock cycle.

Design Tips

To assist you in developing interpretive materials using quotations, passages, and media, design tips are listed below.

- When selecting quotes and passages, consider the reading abilities of the students. Sometimes, reading passage or quotes from different time periods or from other countries can be difficult to read. If quotes or a reading passage are used as an assessment, the reading abilities of the students could affect their score.

- Availability of quotes. Searching online for the quotes about the content taught will yield a variety of options. Other ways to capture quotes is by interviewing your principal, other teachers, or students. Students can determine if the interviewee had any misconceptions or a different perspective about the content. An interview could also be captured on video to show the class.

- Connect to student interests. When possible, relate quotes to students' interests. Often famous celebrities make comments that can connect to the content of class lessons. For example, Lil Wayne, a rap star, stated, "I got ice in my veins, blood in my eyes, hate in my heart, love in my mind." This quote could be integrated to connect to themes or characters in literature and history. Connecting to students' interests and daily experiences reminds students of the current applications of the content.

For steps on designing these types of items, see Figure 6.1.

Figure 6.1 **Steps to Design**

1. Identify a learning target or standard.

2. Search for a quote, passage, or media excerpt that is new to the students and aligns to the standard or learning target.

3. Check to make sure the assessment item is appropriate for the examinees' development, knowledge, skill level, and academic experience.

4. Verify that an assessment item is clear, concise, and focused on the learning target or standard.

5. If the assessment requires an open-ended student response, define the criteria that will be used to evaluate students' responses.

Quotes, Passages, and Media Examples of Tasks and Assessment Examples

This section provides examples of instructional tasks and assessment examples using quotes, passages, and media in the math, science, social studies, and language arts content areas. When reviewing these examples, consider ways you can use these types of interpretive materials in your classroom.

In the multiple-choice questions below, the correct answers are in bold type.

Math Examples

Short Quotes

Example 1:

"My tree house is only 6 feet from my house," Tia told Ashton.

"No, it isn't! It is only 2 yards," Ashton said.

◆ Who is correct? Explain your answer.

_____

_____

_____

_____

Example 2:

"If you think dogs can't count, try putting three dog biscuits in your pocket and then giving Fido only two of them." —Phil Pastoret

Which mathematical operation is discussed in the quote above?

a. addition

b. subtraction

Example 3:

"Your total is $56.73," stated the cashier at the grocery store.

"Here are three twenties," said the customer.

"Your change is $3.37," the cashier said, handing back the change.

◆ Was the amount of change correct? Show your work.

_____

_____

_____

_____

_____

_____

Passages

Example 1:

In _Diary of a Fly_ by Doreen Cronin, Fly's mom says that Fly has 327 brothers and sisters. On June 12 in the book, 87 were stuck to the strip of flypaper. How many of Fly's brothers and sisters were still buzzing around the room? Show all your work.

_____

_____

_____

_____

_____

_____

Example 2:

In _Cook-a-Doodle-Doo!_ by Janet Stevens and Susan Stevens Crummel, Iguana says that 15 minutes equals 900 seconds. If Rooster had to cook the shortcake for 1,680 seconds, how many minutes would that be?

a. 18 minutes

b. 23 minutes

c. 28 minutes

d. 31 minutes

Example 3:

Based on the information from *Teacher at Sea* by Diane Marie Stanitski, imagine that you have discovered a shipwreck and need to measure how deep the ship is in the water. You use the echosounder and the sound pulses return in 6.1 seconds. How deep is the shipwreck? Give your answer in both meters and feet, and show all your work.

_____

_____

_____

Media Clips

Example 1:

How do you use subtraction in your life?

A. Identify a time you used subtraction to solve a real-world problem.

_____

_____

_____

B. Use PhotoPeach (photopeach.com) to create a presentation showing how you solved the problem.

Example 2:

After watching the funny math animation video, describe what is happening to the numbers. Make connections to a mathematical operation.

   Video link: www.youtube.com/watch?v=lnDDf1q6h18

Example 3:

In the song "Geometry Park" by Joe Crone, many shapes are named.

A. On the facing page is a table listing each of the shapes identified in the song. Define and draw a picture of each shape.

B. In groups of three, you are to search the school and our classroom for real-world objects having the shapes listed in the table. Your group should take pictures of the objects showing the shapes. Groups will present their pictures to the class.

Shape	Definition	Picture
Scalene triangle		
Isosceles triangle		
Equilateral triangle		
Hexagon		
Pentagon		
Quadrilateral		
Octagon		
Polygon		

Song: www.songsforteaching.com/geometryparkusa/geometrypark.htm

Example 4:

Based on your understanding from the angle music video, draw a picture of each of the shapes and color red any acute angles, color blue any obtuse angles, and color yellow any right angles.

Shape	Triangle	Square	Octagon	Hexagon
Picture				

Video link: http://youtube/yptZt9hwrzU

Interpretive Exercises: Quotations ◆ 121

Science Examples

Short Quotes

Example 1:

A president once said, "… try, try again." How do scientists use this idea?

  a. Scientists love presidents.

  b. Scientists test many ideas until they get the right answer.

  c. Scientists don't try hard.

Example 2:

"In the Spring, I have counted 136 different kinds of weather inside of 24 hours." —Mark Twain. What characteristic about weather was Mark Twain referring to?

  a. Weather is always changing.

  b. Weather is good in the spring.

  c. Mark Twain liked certain kinds of weather.

  d. Weather only changes a lot in the spring.

Example 3:

"Three things cannot be long hidden: the sun, the moon, and the truth." —Buddha

Based on your knowledge of the sun and the moon, why can't they "be long hidden"?

  a. The sun and moon always rise and set in a regular pattern.

  b. You can always see both the sun and the moon at all times.

  c. Nothing can hide them because nothing is bigger than the sun and the moon.

Passages

Example 1:

Based on your understanding after we read the book *The Reason for a Flower*, complete the following on your flower picture:

A. Cut out and paste the words "roots" and "stem" in the appropriate place on the flower picture.

B. Circle the items on the flower picture that help the flower grow.

Example 2:

We have been learning about the water cycle.

A. Read the poem "Evaporate."

B. Summarize the poem.

C. Create your own poem or rap about one of the stages of the water cycle.

Web link to poem: http://sciencepoems.net/sciencepoems/
evaporate.aspx#.UEfPc41mQvk

Example 3:

We have been discussing the term "natural selection."

A. Read the "Peppered Moth" article.

B. Explain how peppered moths changed colors over time and why.

C. Research another example of natural selection.

D. Prepare a presentation using technology (e.g., Slide Rocket, Prezi, PhotoPeach) that does the following:

◆ Compares your research example of natural selection to the peppered moths.

◆ Explains how this process contributes to the diversity of species.

Web link to article: www.truthinscience.org.uk/tis2/
index.php/component/content/article/127.html

Example 4:

After reading *The Giving Tree*, describe two similarities between the life cycle of the tree and of the boy. Explain two differences between their life cycles.

_____

_____

_____

Media Clips

Example 1:

After watching "Living and Nonliving Things around Us," circle whether each object is living or nonliving.

- Fan   Living   or   **Nonliving**

- Grass   **Living**   or   Nonliving

- Elephant   **Living**   or   Nonliving

- Pen   Living   or   **Nonliving**

- House   Living   or   **Nonliving**

- Tree   **Living**   or   Nonliving

- Bench   Living   or   **Nonliving**

Video link: www.youtube.com/watch?v=lB0WF6P7sSk

Example 2:

After watching the video of volcanic lava, what conclusion can you draw about volcanic eruption?

a. Volcanoes can be classified as a "fast change."

b. Volcanoes produce lava and ash, which both cause changes to the surface of the earth.

c. A volcanic eruption has no visible consequences for the human population.

d. Both A and B

e. All of the above

Video link: www.youtube.com/watch?v=5hE2DZdl0IA

Example 3:

Based on your understandings from watching the physical and chemical changes video, classify the following examples as either a physical or chemical change. Circle the correct answer.

- Dying hair   Physical   or   **Chemical**

- Cooking hamburgers   Physical   or   **Chemical**

- Cutting wood   **Physical**   or   Chemical

- Evaporating water   **Physical**   or   Chemical

- Burning paper   Physical   or   **Chemical**

Video link: www.youtube.com/watch?v=qqqmFFCwd7k.

Social Studies Examples

Short Quotes

Example 1:

"A little matter will move a party, but it must be something great that moves a nation." —Thomas Paine

A. Is the above quote from a primary or secondary source? Explain your answer.

_____

_____

_____

_____

_____

B. What is Thomas Paine referring to when he says, "it must be something great that moves a nation"?

_____

_____

_____

_____

C. What do you think was going on in history to cause Thomas Paine to say this?

_____

_____

_____

_____

_____

Example 2:

Ainsley said in our class yesterday, "I need a bike!" Is that true?

a. Yes, because Ainsley does not have a bike so she needs one.

b. No, because a bike is not a need; it is a want.

c. Yes, because she has been asking for one.

Example 3:

"Darkness cannot drive out darkness; only light can do that. Hate cannot drive out hate; only love can do that." —Martin Luther King Jr.

◆ Describe two actions by Martin Luther King Jr. that carried out his ideas in the statement above.

_____

_____

_____

_____

_____

_____

Passages

Example 1:

Martin Luther King Jr. wrote inspirational speeches.

A. In your groups, read his "I Have a Dream" speech.

B. Go to Wordle (www.wordle.net). Paste in the text of the speech. As a group, examine which words are larger than other words due to their repetition in the text.

C. Select three of the large words in Wordle. Explain why you think Martin Luther King Jr. emphasized each word.

_____

_____

_____

_____

_____

_____

Example 2:

Think about how the characters in the book we read, _The Sneetches_, compromised.

A. Draw a picture of how the characters compromised in the story.

B. On the back of the paper, draw a picture of how you have compromised at school or home.

<u>Example 3:</u>

Think about *The Lorax* story we read.

A. In the first column, draw the natural resource that is central to the story.

B. In the second column, draw a picture of what happened to this natural resource.

C. In the third column, draw a picture of how this natural resource turned into a final product.

Natural resource	What happened next to the natural resource?	Final product

Answer the following questions:

1. Why did the character keep cutting down the trees even though it hurt the environment?

   a. The character wanted to use the trees to make money for his business.

   b. The character used the trees to make his product.

   c. The character did not care about the environment.

   d. All of the above

2. What happened after all the trees were cut down?

   a. Nothing

   b. The character's business was shut down.

   c. All the trees were gone.

   d. Both b and c

3. Should we cut down the trees on our playground to make more room for a baseball field? Explain your answer.

_____

_____

_____

_____

Media Clips

Example 1:

After listening to the song "My Old Kentucky Home," fill out the diagram below. First identify three characteristics about Kentucky that are mentioned in the song. Then describe on the lines provided how those characteristics relate to Kentucky's history.

Characteristic: _____

_____

Describe: _____

_____

_____

_____

_____

_____

Characteristic: _____

_____

Describe: _____

_____

_____

_____

_____

_____

"My Old Kentucky Home"
by Stephen Foster

Characteristic: _____

_____

Describe: _____

_____

_____

_____

_____

_____

Music link: www.youtube.com/watch?v=Dn_ZbX60Oa4

Example 2:

After listening to "The Star-Spangled Banner," consider the ways this song expresses patriotism.

A. Choose one of the three phrases from the song below. Discuss how the phrase from the song represents patriotism.

◆ "Oh, say, does that Star-Spangled Banner yet wave
O'er the land of the free and the home of the brave?"

◆ "Now it catches the gleam of the morning's first beam,
In full glory reflected, now shines in the stream;"

◆ "Blest with vict'ry and peace, may the heav'n rescued land
Praise the Pow'r that hath made and preserved us a nation."

B. In your groups, identify three reasons why this song is played at celebrations and events to represent pride in our country.

Example 3:

We will be researching cultural groups to celebrate their distinctiveness.

A. In your group, chose a cultural group to research. You will be researching the group's language, arts, customs, beliefs, and literature.

B. Find one example for each of the five cultural categories and create an Animoto video (animoto.com/) showcasing the cultural group.

C. Present your video to the class.

D. Each group member should be prepared to explain one similarity between your own life and the life of your cultural group.

Example 4:

After listening to "Follow the Drinking Gourd," answer the following questions:

◆ What is the point of the song?

_____

_____

◆ Why did the slaves decide to put their message into a song?

_____

_____

_____

Song link: www.youtube.com/watch?v=pw6N_eTZP2U

Example 5:

At the beginning of the video "Sesame Street: Cookie Monster and Count Cooperate," the Count and the Cookie Monster argue. This is called what?

a. conflict

b. cooperation

How did the Count and the Cookie Monster cooperate? Give an example of a time when you cooperated with someone.

_____

_____

_____

_____

_____

_____

_____

_____

Video link: www.youtube.com/watch?v=5l7KbMVdN7E

Language Arts Examples

Short Quotes

Example 1:

A Jewish folk saying states, "Don't ask questions of fairy tales."

A. What do you think this statement means?

_____

_____

_____

B. How does this apply to Ella's marriage to Prince Charming in *Just Ella* by Margaret Peterson Haddix?

_____

_____

_____

_____

Example 2:

In our story *Diary of a Fly*, the fly states, "Things they should teach you in flight class: Always have a flight plan." Which quote do you think he would agree with?

a. "Take a chance."

b. "Be prepared."

c. "Don't think."

Example 3:

Tom Bradley said, "A loving, caring teacher took a liking to me. She noticed the potential and wanted to help shape it."

A. Does this quote describe Ms. Plum in the book we just read, *The Magical Ms. Plum*? Why or why not?

_____

_____

_____

_____

B. Using the Big Huge Labs website (bighugelabs.com), find a picture that looks like Ms. Plum in your imagination and put a caption below it showing something that she might say to you.

_____

_____

_____

_____

Passages

Example 1:

After reading *The Lorax*, by Dr. Seuss, answer the three questions posed at the beginning of the story.

◆ "What *was* the Lorax?" _____

◆ "And why was it there?" _____

◆ "And why was it lifted and taken somewhere _____
   _____

From the far end of town where the Grickle-grass grows?"

From *The Lorax* by Dr. Seuss

Example 2:

"In my garden, the flowers could change color

Just by my thinking about it—

Pink, blue, green, purple. Even patterns."

From *My Garden* by Kevin Henkes

Circle the color that the speaker does **NOT** say:

   a. pink

   b. blue

   c. yellow

   d. green

Example 3:

In *The Red Badge of Courage*,

   A. Describe how Henry responds when the conflict heightens.

   _____

   _____

   _____

   B. If you were a soldier in a war today, do you think that you would do
       the same? Criticize or defend Henry's decision.

   _____

   _____

   _____

   C. Post your answers to part B on the website page that I created on
       Wallwisher (wallwisher.com).

   _____

   _____

   _____

   D. Examine the different ideas presented by other groups and move the
       online posts around to group similar ideas.

   _____

   _____

   _____

Media Clips

Example 1:

In *Fever 1793*, we read about a young woman's response to the yellow fever outbreak in Philadelphia. Based on the "A Taste of History" video, circle all of the following items that show how people of the time reacted to the sickness.

a. They avoided infected people.

b. They used bloodletting to "cure" patients.

c. They kept streets clean.

d. They built more churches.

Video link: www.youtube.com/watch?v=jSr2gwInkKU

Example 2:

We just read *Nim's Island*.

A. Choose one of Nim's animal friends.

B. Go to *National Geographic*'s website and find a video about your animal.

C. Fill out the chart below to show what your animal needs.

My animal is _____. It needs _____.

Food	
Water	
Shelter	

Example 3:
We just read *Bone #1: Out From Boneville*.

A. Find a song that reminds you of the story.

_____

_____

_____

B. Explain three similarities between the song and the story.

_____

_____

_____

_____

_____

_____

Discuss

◆ How are other teachers in your school using quotes, passages, and media in instructional tasks and assessments?

◆ In your classroom, how could you effectively integrate quotes, passages, and media to increase higher-level thinking?

Take Action

◆ Design an instructional task or assessment using a quote, passage, and/or media item.

◆ Examine the instructional tasks and assessments you currently use. Where could you replace an instructional task or assessment with a quote, passage, and/or media item to improve instructional quality?

Establishing a Culture of Thinking

Critical thinking must, therefore, command a place in any institution committed to the pursuit of education because critical thinking is a necessary condition of it.

—J.E. McPeck

To establish a culture of thinking in your classroom or school, teaching must transition from memorization to deeper applications of knowledge. Graphics, scenarios, and quotes provide a clear way of incorporating cognitively demanding instructional tasks and assessments. For many teachers, their own K–12 experience did not include deep thinking experiences. To build a culture of thinking, teachers must embrace different instructional practices that nurture cognitive development.

Thinking is a skill that can be taught to all students. Teachers must intentionally plan cognitively demanding experiences in order for students to practice and develop their thinking capacities. When critical thinking is embedded in classroom instruction, students experience a rich array of opportunities that inherently develop their capacity to process information on higher levels. This chapter will discuss ways to establish a classroom culture that supports thinking and will recommend possible ways to incorporate interpretive exercises into formative and summative assessments.

Classroom Culture That Nurtures Thinking: Training the Brain

Classrooms can be work cultures or thinking cultures. Work cultures emphasize students completing assignments, but often at a low cognitive level. However, thinking cultures nurture students' thinking skills (Ritchhart, 2002). As Michael Michalko (2011) notes,

> We went to school. We were not taught how to think; we were taught to reproduce what past thinkers thought. ... Instead of being taught to look for possibilities, we were taught to exclude them. It's as if we entered school as a question mark and graduated as a period. (p. 3)

Classrooms should encourage student questions and inquiries; student thinking should be the heart of the classroom.

There are several ways a teacher can purposefully enhance the enculturation of thinking: creating a physical environment promoting thinking, modeling the thinking process, teaching routines and structures for thinking, providing thinking opportunities, establishing clear expectations for thinking, and building supportive relationships to build thinking skills (Ritchhart, 2002). Just as people go to a gym to train their bodies to be stronger and more agile, teachers can train brains in a *thought-full* classroom.

Organize the Physical Environment

The physical environment of a gym can attract new customers. Some gyms post positive statements promoting fitness and strategically arrange the facility to better meet the needs of their customers. Similarly, the physical environment of the classroom can be organized to engage the brain. The visual cues and setup of the room can establish the importance of thinking. Posting high-level questions starters, as provided in the second chapter of this book, around the room prompts teachers and students to pose higher-level questions. Posters with engaging images and quotes can ignite student thinking. For example, the common quote, "Neurons that fire together wire together" can be an opening topic of conversation at the beginning of the school year. As students enter the room, the teacher can post a controversial question or quote for the current unit to immediately spark students' thinking about the content. For each unit, central questions such as "Is America progressing as a nation?" will challenge students to develop an overarching understanding of the lessons. The teacher can also list on the board lingering questions students have about the topics studied. This practice emphasizes that teachers do not have all the answers, but seek to deepen their understandings as well. Teachers can also designate a special lounge chair in the classroom for the "Thinker of the Day," celebrating a student who posed or answered a deep thinking question that day. Honoring good thinking should be a regular occurrence in thinking classrooms.

Establish the Importance of Critical Thinking Skills

When exercising, personal trainers and exercise instructors emphasize how a particular exercise benefits the body so their clients will understand the significance of the exercise. Likewise, at the beginning of the school year, students need to understand the reasons why critical thinking is important. The teacher can ask the class to generate a list of reasons why critical thinking would be imperative to their future success; students can then discuss the reasons why critical thinking is vital for personal and career success, as noted in the first chapter of this text. Just as teachers need to understand the reason for teaching thinking skills, students need to understand the positive effects of thinking. By establishing a focus on thinking, teachers can transform classrooms from mass-production classrooms with students able to answer fact-based questions to classrooms that embody real learning through thinking as students analyze, critique, and create.

Communicate Expectations for Thinking

When developing an exercise plan in the gym, clients identify their health goals. This establishes a target, whether it is to lose body fat or increase their level of activity. In the same way, students need clear thinking expectations. Grading criteria and models of student work should be shared with students. As students become more aware of their level of critical thinking, they should be encouraged to self-evaluate their performance based on the scoring guidelines. At the end of this chapter there is a critical thinking rubric that can be used to assess the level of thinking on an assignment (see Take Action, Figure 7.4). Before submitting their final product, students can self- and peer-assess their work based on the rubric, which teaches students to evaluate. In giving supportive and specific feedback during the peer assessment, student reviewers can helpfully point out revisions to their partner's work and often realize changes to be made in their own work. When instructional tasks move from memorizing to thinking, often a different type of student is more successful in your class—a deep thinker.

Establish Routines and Structures for Thinking

Some gyms help members design an exercise plan indicating the exact exercises that will be completed each week. Students need similar supports to organize their thinking. A thinking routine is a thinking strategy that has a few steps that are easy to teach and learn. This strategy can be used in a variety of contexts. Once a thinking routine is taught, it should be practiced frequently to develop competency. Several thinking routines and thinking structures are described along with the steps to implement the routine.

Numbered Heads

Students discuss questions in groups before the teacher asks questions. Students do not know whom the teacher will select so all students are prepared to answer.

1. The teacher divides students into groups and gives each group member a number.

2. The teacher poses a thoughtful question.

3. Groups discuss the answer.

4. The teacher calls a number and the person in each group with that number must respond to the question.

Think-Pair-Share

This routine gives students time to think individually before giving an answer, which is particularly helpful when higher-level thinking questions are posed (Lyman, 1981).

1. A question is posed.

2. Students individually think about the question and record their initial thoughts and/or answer.

3. Students share their thoughts with a partner.

4. Partners share their thoughts with the class.

Graphic Organizer/Concepts Map

Graphic organizers and concepts maps are another way for students to organize their thinking. Venn diagrams, flow charts, idea wheels, problem-solution charts, word webs, story maps, sequence charts, time lines, time-order charts, and persuasion maps are just some of the many types of organizers.

When teachers embed thinking routines into classroom instruction, students become active constructors of meaning. Learning begins with the students' thoughts as they develop their own initial ideas through the prompting of the questions in the thinking routines or the graphic organizer. These routines and the graphic organizers may be used in a group setting, which promotes sharing of diverse ideas and questions (Ritchhart, Palmer, Church, & Tishman, 2006). When teachers use certain routines or structures for thinking, they should use the name of the skill or routine to trigger the application—for instance, by saying "Evaluate ..." instead of "What are the positive aspects of ...?" This encourages students to become familiar with the language.

Model Thinking Aloud

Many gyms provide staff to demonstrate to new members how to use the exercise equipment. Additionally, in exercise classes, teachers will model the appropriate way to complete the exercise. In classrooms, students need teachers to explain their thinking aloud so students become aware of the thinking processes involved in high-level thinking tasks. When interpretive exercises or high-level questions are first introduced, the teacher should model how to approach the question. Explicit modeling and making thinking visible to students has been shown to improve students' thinking processes (Ritchhart & Perkins, 2008). More direct approaches may be particularly important for struggling students. Students with few successful experiences thinking on higher levels will find teacher modeling particularly helpful as they see how expert thinkers reason. In addition, students can share their thinking processes with each other in groups to describe how they arrived at their conclusions or answers. Understanding other people's thinking can help students reflect on their own thinking.

Provide Thinking Opportunities

To become physically fit, people must devote time to exercising. Just as in learning any new skill, with more time and opportunities, students will become more capable thinkers. If students are to become proficient thinkers, curriculum must focus on thinking, classrooms must be student-centered, developmentally appropriate practices must be followed, and students should learn to use their thinking skills in many different contexts.

Curriculum Focus on Thinking

In order to be better thinkers, students must have time to think. Schools must weed out some of the low-level curriculum, activities, and assessments that are not necessary and replace them with higher-level thinking tasks. Kurfiss (1988) states, "The characteristically American view that there is not 'time' to allow students to think has probably done considerable damage to learning" (p. 71). Schools need to build depth of understanding instead of focusing solely on covering a myriad of topics. Critical thinking learning tasks require more instructional time but produce more lasting learning since students will gain a deeper understanding by completing them. It might mean selecting fewer concepts and teaching them to greater depths of understanding.

To allow students to see the broader concepts, teachers can structure lessons around themes, such as justice, change, power, patterns, conflict, forces, compromise, relationships, or passion.

Student-Centered Thinking

Thinking opportunities should be student-centered. If used correctly, classroom discussions are a perfect opportunity for students to engage in debate. Paul and Elder (2007) caution teachers, "Speak less so they can think more" (p. 44). Sometimes in classroom discussions teachers make most of the comments. Other times, the teacher poses deep thinking questions only to go ahead and answer the question aloud without giving students time to process their answer. In order to develop a critical manner, students should be encouraged to question each other. Teachers with thinking classrooms are willing to tolerate ambiguity and learn to suspend judgment as students develop their reasons. In a student-centered thinking classroom, the teacher is not seen as the source of all information or the determiner of the "correct answer." The teacher asks questions rather than telling information—a collaborative partnership in inquiry. Divergent opinions and thoughts are encouraged, and teachers should refrain from telling their own opinions lest they stifle the students' thinking processes.

Teachers can build lessons around questions, problems, and case studies to encourage active, experiential learning when students' natural curiosities are awakened. When students are deeply involved in a task and are willing to expend a large amount of effort to understand concepts or learn a skill, this is termed cognitive engagement (Boykin & Noguera, 2011). When teachers incorporate choices in the task and appeal to students' learning preferences, it increases the potential for cognitive engagement (Tishman, 2001). Thinking classrooms are full of challenge opportunities, student choice, and tasks that pique students' curiosity (Diamond & Hopson, 1999).

Developmentally Appropriate Practices

When designing thinking experiences, teachers should consider students' previous experiences and developmental levels. Posing a thought-provoking challenge allows teachers to assess the level of the students' thinking in order to establish a baseline of their current abilities. Baseline assessments can help teachers and students track the development of their critical thinking skills. In addition, baseline assessments give the teacher information on students' current abilities so as not to overestimate or underestimate students' skill levels. Based on students' current abilities, teachers can then set realistic expectations for students to develop their thinking skills. Tasks should provide an appropriate balance of challenge and support. If tasks are beyond the skill level of the students and the teacher does not give sufficient support, the students may become overwhelmed and produce poor work. Teachers may become disillusioned and revert to low-level thinking activities to improve the students' level of success. On the other hand, if tasks are not sufficiently challenging, students may lack motivation to produce quality work. Teachers should select critical thinking tasks that challenge students to advance their abilities one step further. By scaffolding experiences to meet the individual needs of the student, teachers can help students gain a better sense of self-efficacy and become more motivated to tackle other thinking tasks (Lynch, Wolcott, & Huber, 2001). Gradually teachers should remove the scaffolds so students can independently complete thinking tasks.

Applying Thinking Skills in Multiple Contexts

Issues arise in the school and classroom that empower students to use thinking routines and devise a solution. For example, the class could work together and use the decision-making framework to solve a classroom management problem. Students often have difficulty applying thinking skills in contexts other than where they learned them. Using thinking skills to address classroom or school problems helps students learn to apply thinking routines and skills in many different contexts. Additionally, teachers can have students brainstorm a list of other situations where they could use the thinking skills practiced in the classroom in order to facilitate transfer of these abilities to different contexts.

Supportive Relationships and Interactions to Promote Thinking

To help a gym's clients reach their health goals, exercise instructors build positive relationships with the clients. With established relationships, exercise instructors can offer positive and helpful feedback to continually nudge clients toward their goals. When teachers build supportive relationships that promote thinking, students will be more willing to try difficult tasks. Clearly a teacher's negative response to student questions would inhibit critical thinking (Buck, 2002). Teachers should celebrate when students obviously have engaged in sophisticated thought processes. This might be through a verbal reinforcement—"Kiss your brain!" where students kiss their hand and then touch their head—or through a nonverbal response like a fist bump or a pat on the shoulder. I remember when a student who struggled in my class did exceptionally well on an open-ended response assessment. I asked the student to stay after class for a moment and then told him we were going to the office. There I asked him to call his parents. After dialing, he anxiously handed me the phone, probably remembering his frequent calls to his parents about disciplinary infractions. I told his mother in front of him that he had done extraordinarily well on an assessment by citing specific examples to support each point. I told her that I was extremely proud of his effort and structured thinking. His mother was thrilled and the boy smiled from ear to ear. Who doesn't like to hear good things about themselves?

Figure 7.1 **Feedback to Promote Student Thinking**

Feedback to Promote Student Thinking
◆ Affirm student's thinking. "Your ideas are important for us to hear."
◆ Ask for clarification. "Could you help me understand … ?"
◆ Request for elaboration. "Please tell us more about your thinking on this."
◆ Share feelings. "How did that make you feel?"
◆ Reflect on the thinking. "How did you come to that solution or conclusion?"
◆ Pursue reasoning. "What evidence supports your conclusions?"
◆ Inquire about opposing evidence. "What evidence doesn't support your conclusion or point of view?"
◆ Apply ideas. "How have you used this knowledge in other areas of your life?"
◆ Reflect. "What have you learned?"

Source: Costa, A. (Ed.). (2001). *Developing minds: A resource book for teaching thinking,* 3rd ed., pp. 108–109. Alexandria, VA: ASCD. © 2001 by ASCD. Reprinted with permission. Learn more about ASCD at www.ascd.org.

When teachers encourage students and provide growth-oriented feedback, it can advance student thinking (Dweck, 2006). Constructive feedback focused on the connection between a student's ability and positive outcomes most likely will result in increased perceived self-efficacy and a tendency to seek out additional challenges (Bandura, 1997). Feedback should promote thinking by giving students specific ways they can improve their work (see Figure 7.1). If students think that their ideas will be rejected, they will be less likely to offer ideas. Teachers who respond negatively or allow other students to do so or cut off students when answering will reduce students' participation. Teachers should focus not on the right answer but on identifying how students arrived at the answer.

Several conditions have been identified for establishing a thinking climate during class discussions. Teachers must listen carefully to students, showing respect for students and their ideas. When teachers and students listen and exchange ideas, the teacher-student relationship morphs into a partnership for learning, both learning from each other. By establishing a safe climate for ideas, teachers encourage students to pose questions and consider alternative viewpoints and ideas.

Another way to support students is through group work. Ritchhart & Perkins (2008) state that "the development of thinking is a social endeavor" (p. 58). Many of the thinking routines include opportunities to discuss with a partner or small group. Through the use of group work, students can engage in collaborative problem-solving and consider different perspectives. Group members can expose false assumptions and flawed thinking that someone individually might not recognize. Collaboration promotes conflict resolution, which requires thinking skills.

To encourage a thinking culture, students should be involved in decision-making processes in the organization of classrooms. For example, the class can design a plan to address the situation of peers inappropriately using the restrooms or working in groups. When teachers involve students in the decision-making of the classroom, it establishes a cooperative environment and gives students opportunities to apply their thinking skills to various contexts.

Finally, teachers should encourage students to learn from their mistakes and consider failure a part of the learning process. After failing, students should reflect on what went wrong and what they can do differently next time. Teachers should provide multiple opportunities for students to demonstrate their skills and understandings so students can improve their work.

Formatively Assessing Thinking

There are many ways to formatively assess thinking with engaging techniques. Marzano (2011) notes that if we "increase the number of students who respond we increase the chances of the information moving into working memory" (p. 12). To engage students in thinking about interpretive exercises, numerous strategies will be presented.

Strategies

Below is a list of some ways to formatively assess students' thinking.

- **Bell Ringer:** I strongly advocate that when students switch classes there should be a bell ringer question on the board to engage students in content immediately. Bell ringers with interpretive exercises are a great way for a teacher to immediately engage students in the content as they enter the classroom. Bell ringers could review information from the day before or preassess students' knowledge of a topic.

- **Exit Ticket:** At the end of class, students respond to a question on a paper or index card to check their understanding of the lesson. The teacher can use the information to form differentiated groups the next day based on students' different levels of understanding.

- **Guess What?** At the beginning of class, a graphic, quote, or scenario is posed. Students then guess what they will be learning about that day.

- **Four Corners:** After students examine the introductory information in an interpretive exercise, a teacher poses a question and gives an A, B, C, or D answer choice. Students move to the corner designated for the answer choice they believe is the best answer. In the corners the group members discuss their answer. After a class discussion, the students can switch corners if they feel they need to change their answer.

- **Agree or Disagree:** As in Four Corners, the students examine the interpretive exercises and the teacher poses a controversial question. The room is divided in half and students stand on either side of the room depending on their answer. The class then engages in a debate about the question.

- **ABCD Cards:** Each student holds four cards, each printed with A, B, C, or D. The teacher poses a multiple-choice question and students answer by raising the appropriate card. Teachers can quickly collect formative assessment data on students' understanding of the content while giving students an opportunity to engage in a bodily-kinesthetic activity.

- **Classroom Response Systems:** Classroom response systems or clickers are a technological way to do the same thing as the ABCD cards. More sophisticated, this technology allows the teacher and/or class to view a data display showing how many students indicated each answer.

- **Computer or Cell Phone Polls:** For those who do not have a classroom response system, students can use computers or cell phones to answer multiple-choice or open-ended questions. Websites like Poll Daddy, Poll Everywhere, and Wiffiti provide free services for this activity.

- **True/False Cards:** Just as students use the ABCD cards, students can use cards labeled True or False. The teacher reads a statement and students raise their card to indicate if the statement is true or false. The teacher can then ask why the statement is false.

- **True/Not True/True with Modification/Unable to Determine:** More advanced learners can classify a statement into one of four categories: True, Not True, True with Modification, or Unable to Determine (Himmele & Himmele, 2009). After students indicate their answer, the class could discuss reasons for voting for each option. A variation is for groups to work together to classify statements and then share their thoughts with the class.

- **Dry-Erase Boards:** Students respond to interpretive exercises with short answers on individual dry-erase boards. A cheaper method is giving students a sheet protector with a dry-erase marker.

- **Online Thought Boards:** Teachers pose an interpretive question and students respond online through Internet sites such as Wallwisher and Lino It. Answers can then be categorized by grouping ideas on the online board.

- **Question Cube:** Students make a cube using online patterns with question starters for each side, such as "What consequence might happen if …?" or "Can you compare …?" Working in groups, students roll the cube and make a question using the starter. The group then discusses the answer to that question.

- **Students Write the Questions:** Groups formulate questions to ask other groups. Groups then exchange questions and answer the questions they've been given. For each thoughtful question or response to a question, groups can move a token to the center of their desk. This can be a game to accumulate as many tokens as possible by asking or answering questions thoughtfully.

- **Questioning Starters:** Use the question starter guide in the second chapter of this book to help you ask higher-level questions. There are also iPad and iPhone applications, including Stick Pick, which can help you track the questioning in your class. This application prompts you with question starters and can help you differentiate your question starters to different abilities in the class.

- **Graffiti Wall:** Teachers post interpretive exercises around the room along with questions and blank chart paper. Students move individually or in groups to each interpretive exercise and record answers to the questions, post questions, or add thoughts. Students are expected to add new insights on the chart paper near each interpretive exercise. Individuals or groups can use different color markers to identify their contributions.

- **Mystery:** The teacher gives groups several introductory materials and asks students to make inferences about what is happening. For example, to learn about an author, the students might be given quotes by the author, pictures of the covers of the author's books, and a news article. From all of these sources, the groups determine the best conclusions that can be made about the author. Also, the teacher could provide various introductory materials and ask groups to select only three to use. This would challenge students to really think about which materials would provide the most information on the author.

- **Inductive Learning:** Inductive learning involves giving groups five to eight introductory materials and having them classify them into larger categories that the students have to determine. For instance, students could be given visuals, real-world examples, and quotes about the water cycle and then decide how to categorize these materials into larger groups. Groups might determine that the items all dealt with two parts of the water cycle: condensation and evaporation.

Think Time

With higher-level items, it is important that students are given time to think. The traditional three- to five-second window for think time needs to be dramatically extended to provide time for students to process the information and determine an answer. In fact, a simple test I use to determine if the question is higher-level is to think about how long it would take me to formulate an answer. If I can do it quickly, it is probably a lower-level question.

To prevent the fastest hand in the class from answering all the questions, a teacher could randomly select students by instituting a No Hands Up rule. With No Hands Up, the teacher records the student's names on craft sticks or slips of paper. An easy way is to make a copy of the student roster, cut apart the names, and place them in an envelope. The teacher poses the question and selects a name from the envelope or sticks to determine who gets the question. Teachers can also use online or smartphone applications like Stick Pick to randomly select students. This method of selecting students for questions keeps all students engaged because they never know who will be picked to answer the question. To encourage students to pose questions to each other, the teacher can randomly select another student to answer the question posed.

If a student is called on and does not know the answer, the teacher might offer hints or let the student get assistance from a friend. However, to ensure that the called-on student understands, the student should be asked to summarize what was mentioned or add on to the answer given.

Differentiating

Bloom's taxonomy works seamlessly with differentiation. The teacher can pose an assignment about a given topic and provide options at different levels of the taxonomy. For example, after discussing political platforms, students could either (a) choose the ideas out of either of the political parties' platforms to design a platform that represents their views (Analyze/Evaluate level), or (b) create a new political platform that represents ideas for a new political party (Create level). Both options show high expectations, but they are differentiated to challenge all learners. Scholastic rigor is for all, and learning is enhanced when there is an appropriate level of challenge offered to students.

Real-World Interests

Students will be more interested in engaging in thinking activities when they connect to students' real-life experiences and interests (Ritchhart & Perkins, 2008). Teachers should select graphics, scenarios, and quotes that will engage the class in issues, problems, and practical situations that are appealing. If you are unsure of your students' interests, ask them. Many students are interested in sports, music, and media. Almost any topic can be connected to lyrics of songs. Sports and media also can be integrated into many subject areas. Making classroom connections to a wide variety of students' passions allows students to link information in new ways while appealing to students' interests.

Along with interests, teachers should allow student choice. Students might choose between two different tasks or select materials from any media to support their opinion. Any time students are given a choice, they tend to be more motivated to complete the task.

Summative Assessments

Interpretive exercises can be included in summative assessments using a variety of formats. Teachers can use the exercises to prompt students' thinking. Students would then develop various products demonstrating the students' ability to Analyze, Evaluate, and Create, the top three levels of Bloom's revised taxonomy (Anderson & Krathwohl, 2001). Interpretive exercises can also be used in more traditional formats like multiple-choice assessments or open-ended writing tasks.

Students can use their understanding of interpretive exercises to design a variety of products, such as web pages, songs, museum exhibits, landscape designs, or new recipes. Often, assignments that produce a product work well with authentic tasks.

Critical thinking skills can also be assessed in traditional formats, including multiple-choice and open-ended writing tasks. On a test, an interpretive exercise could include multiple questions to be answered based on one interpretive item. When used in this manner, often each subsequent question addresses a higher level of complexity. Below are some ways that interpretive exercises can be integrated into assessments in a multiple-choice format.

- ◆ **Conclusion Follows/Conclusion Does Not Follow:** After interpretative materials are presented, a conclusion is stated with three multiple-choice options: (a) The conclusion follows; (b) The conclusion does not follow; or (c) The conclusion is partially supported by the evidence.

  - ◇ Example: Based on the chart provided, more females than males failed the test.
    - a. The conclusion follows.
    - b. The conclusion does not follow.
    - c. The conclusion is partially supported by the evidence.

- ◆ **Generalization:** A generalization is reasoning from detailed facts to general principles. Students are asked to make a generalization or determine which generalization can be made from an interpretive exercise. Students select "S" if the statement is supported by the data, "R" if the statement is refuted by the data, or "N" if the statement is neither supported nor refuted by the data (Gronlund, 2006, p. 104).

  - ◇ Example: Based on the passage provided, bullying at the high school caused several fights. Circle the correct answer: S, R, N

- ◆ **Support/Oppose:** After reviewing interpretive information, students are asked to choose if provided statements support or oppose the author's hypothesis.

- ◆ **Relevant Arguments:** After reading a passage, quote, scenario, or real-world example or listening to a media clip, students classify arguments posed as either relevant or irrelevant.

Interpretive exercises can also be used with essay and open-ended assessments, as shown in the examples in this text. With the four options above, students can choose the correct answer and then justify their answer in writing.

Summary

Building a culture of thinking in a classroom takes an intentional effort. A classroom culture that nurtures high cognitive demand includes a physical environment that promotes thinking, a clear priority to improve critical thinking skills, developed routines and structures for thinking, teacher modeling of appropriate thinking practices, multiple and well-suited thinking opportunities, communicated expectations for thinking, and supportive relationships and interactions to promote thinking. When teachers use formative assessments with interpretive exercises to measure students' thinking abilities, they should utilize multiple formative assessment strategies, provide sufficient thinking time, differentiate, and connect to students' real-world interests. Summative assessments with interpretive exercises can be project-oriented, open-ended, or include forced-choice assessments like multiple-choice questions.

Discuss

◆ How do you currently support a thinking culture in your school or classroom?

◆ What are some ways to enhance the thinking culture in your school or classroom?

◆ What metaphor would characterize a thinking classroom?

Take Action

◆ Evaluate the level of thinking in your classroom by using Figure 7.2, "Elements of a Classroom Culture That Nurtures Thinking." Circle the items in the table that are part of your classroom practice.

◆ Review the thinking routines in this chapter. Select one and implement it in your classroom.

◆ A critical thinking rubric (Figure 7.3) is included at the end of this chapter. When can you use this rubric to assess your students' critical thinking?

Figure 7.2 **Elements of a Classroom Culture That Nurtures Thinking**

Elements of a Classroom Culture That Nurtures Thinking
Physical Environment
✓ Visual cues (e.g., posters, questions posted on the wall) promote thinking
✓ Organization of the room promotes thinking
Establish the Importance of Critical Thinking Skills
✓ Early in the school year, students can clearly state the reasons for critical thinking
Communicate Expectations for Thinking
✓ Grading criteria for thinking tasks are explained to students
✓ Models of student work are shared with students
✓ Students self-evaluate their work based on thinking criteria
✓ Peer assessment is used with thinking tasks
Routines and Structures for Thinking
✓ Thinking routines are taught and regularly practiced
Teacher Modeling
✓ Teacher models thinking
Thinking Opportunities
✓ Students are given many opportunities to refine their thinking abilities
✓ Curriculum focuses on deep understandings
✓ Students question each other
✓ Divergent opinions and thoughts are encouraged
✓ Thinking tasks appeal to students' learning preferences and curiosity and provide student choice
✓ Pre-assessments measure students' abilities in order to determine appropriate tasks
✓ Students apply thinking skills in multiple contexts
Supportive Relationships and Interactions to Promote Thinking
✓ Student questions are encouraged
✓ Teacher provides appropriate feedback
✓ Students are engaged in collaborative tasks
✓ Students are involved in the classroom decision-making process
✓ Teacher supports learning from mistakes

Figure 7.3 **Holistic Scoring Guide**

The Holistic Critical Thinking Scoring Rubric
A Tool for Developing and Evaluating Critical Thinking

Strong 4—Consistently does all or almost all of the following:

- Accurately interprets evidence, statements, graphics, questions, etc.
- Identifies the most important arguments (reasons and claims) pro and con.
- Thoughtfully analyzes and evaluates major alternative points of view.
- Draws warranted, judicious, non-fallacious conclusions.
- Justifies key results and procedures, explains assumptions and reasons.
- Fair-mindedly follows where evidence and reasons lead.

Acceptable 3—Does most or many of the following:

- Accurately interprets evidence, statements, graphics, questions, etc.
- Identifies relevant arguments (reasons and claims) pro and con.
- Offers analyses and evaluations of obvious alternative points of view.
- Draws warranted, non-fallacious conclusions.
- Justifies some results or procedures, explains reasons.
- Fair-mindedly follows where evidence and reasons lead.

Unacceptable 2—Does most or many of the following:

- Misinterprets evidence, statements, graphics, questions, etc.
- Fails to identify strong, relevant counter-arguments.
- Ignores or superficially evaluates obvious alternative points of view.
- Draws unwarranted or fallacious conclusions.
- Justifies few results or procedures, seldom explains reasons.
- Regardless of the evidence or reasons, maintains or defends views based on self-interest or preconceptions.

Weak 1—Consistently does all or almost all of the following:

- Offers biased interpretations of evidence, statements, graphics, questions, information, or the points of view of others.
- Fails to identify or hastily dismisses strong, relevant counter-arguments.
- Ignores or superficially evaluates obvious alternative points of view.
- Argues using fallacious or irrelevant reasons, and unwarranted claims.
- Does not justify results or procedures, nor explain reasons.
- Regardless of the evidence or reasons, maintains or defends views based on self-interest or preconceptions.
- Exhibits close-mindedness or hostility to reason.

Source: From P. Facione & N.C. Facione. (1994). *Holistic critical thinking scoring rubric.*
Reprinted with permission of California Academic Press.

Conclusion

8

Some people study all their life and at their death they have learned everything except to THINK.

—François-Urbain Domergue

It is 2:30 p.m. on the last day of school, and the buses will roll out of the parking lot at 3 p.m. The school counselor announces that money has been stolen from her purse—$300 in cash. Is the culprit a student or a staff member? With no previous instances of stealing in the front office, it seems improbable that this is a staff issue. Teachers and other staff were attending the awards ceremony in the gym, leaving few people in the office. A secretary comments that she had caught a student at 11 a.m. looking around my office, the principal's office, and told him to go back to class. After considering the possible hypotheses, we agree that a student roaming in the front office while administrators were at an awards ceremony seems a likely suspect. Another office worker mentions that she had observed the same student in the counselor's office at 11:30 a.m. and told him to go to class. With two accounts from two reliable witnesses, the evidence seems to point toward the roaming student. Staff members find him in class—it is 2:45 p.m. He denies the charge and his belongings are searched. No evidence of the money is found.

It is five minutes until the buses arrive. The choices are to send the student home on the bus or retain him for further questioning. A decision is made, based on two credible eyewitness testimonies of suspicious behavior in the front office, that the student should be detained. When a teacher, a school counselor, and the principal try to extract the truth, the student again denies the charge. Parents and then police are called. The parent warns the student to tell the truth to the police officer. After a one-hour discussion with the police officer, the student admits that he stole the money and reveals its hiding place—between the cushions in the front-office couch.

With thirty minutes left on the clock on our last day, I had to make a quick, thoughtful decision in this situation. First, I had to understand the situation by gathering information from all sources. In this case, a student

◆ 151

was going to be investigated, and I needed to consider whether the information was from a reliable source. Ultimately, by 2:45, I had to make a decision whether there was sufficient evidence to continue questioning him or whether I should let him go home on the bus, knowing that, since this was the last school day of the year, it would be difficult to talk to him again and if he had stolen the money it would probably never be recovered.

This is real life—convoluted and complicated. Our students, currently and in their future careers and life situations, encounter similar problematic issues. We as educators have the power to equip them with skills to handle these situations thoughtfully and make good decisions. The job will necessitate letting go of some tasks and assessments that require little thinking, while challenging students to be 21st-century learners as they wade into the complex issues of the content areas you teach. Henry Ford said, "Thinking is hard work, and that's why so few people do it."

Through this text I have tried to make a case for the importance of critical thinking. Misconceptions regarding thinking were addressed, and a detailed description of Bloom's revised taxonomy was provided. To help educators design higher-level thinking tasks and assessments, interpretive exercises were presented as one way to meet that need. Scenarios, real-world examples, and authentic tasks provide a method to assess students in a close to real-world context. Visuals, including illustrations, maps, diagrams, data tables, and charts, appeal to visual learners while also engaging them in higher-level thinking. Short quotes, passages, and media clips are another approach to challenge students to understand, analyze, and evaluate information. Finally, the text showcased ways to build a thinking culture in a classroom along with formative and summative assessment ideas.

The intention of this text is to enhance teachers' understanding of high-level thinking tasks and assessments. Now it is time for action. The first step is for teachers to assess the level of thinking in their classroom and select several ideas in this text that they can apply immediately. An Implementation Chart (Figure 8.1) is included at the end of this chapter to help teachers make a plan.

Thinking skills will equip students for college, work, and daily life. By building a classroom culture that supports thinking, teachers can prime their students for all these experiences. Thanks to these efforts, students will be prepared to meet the challenges and changes in our century with success.

Discuss

- ◆ What are three ideas in the text you can immediately implement?
- ◆ What statements in the text have been most helpful in improving your professional practices?

Take Action

◆ Complete the Implementation Chart (Figure 8.1). Indicate your specific goals, how you will measure them, and the time frame for completing them.

◆ Identify another teacher, perhaps one who is in a professional learning community with you. Share your implementation goals, and agree on a date when you will meet to consider evidence of completing the goals. After you have implemented your goals, meet with your colleague and consider evidence of how you executed your plan. Discuss successes, ways to improve, and next steps you can take to continue enhancing the thinking skills in your classroom.

Figure 8.1 **Implementation Chart**

Specific Goal	Measure	Time Frame
Example: *I will include visual interpretive exercises at the beginning of class (bell ringers) to improve my students' higher-level thinking skills.*	*I will assess student performance on these items weekly.*	*I will do this daily during the first quarter of the semester.*

References

Achieve. (2006). *Closing the expectations gap 2006: An annual 50-state progress report on the alignment of high school policies with the demands of college and work.* Retrieved from www.achieve.org/files/50-state-06-Final.pdf.

ACT. (2006). *Ready to succeed: All students prepared for college and work.* Retrieved from www.act.org/research/policymakers/pdf/ready_to_succeed.pdf.

ACT. (2011). *The condition of college and career readiness 2011.* Retrieved from www.act.org/readiness/2011.

Anderson, L. W., & Krathwohl, D. R. (Eds.). (2001). *A taxonomy for learning, teaching, and assessing: A revision of Bloom's* Taxonomy of Educational Objectives (complete edition). New York: Longman.

Bandura, A. (1997). *Self-efficacy: The exercise of control.* New York: W. H. Freeman.

Blackburn, B. R. (2008). *Rigor is not a four-letter word.* New York: Eye On Education.

Bloom, B. S. (Ed.). (1956). *Taxonomy of educational objectives: The classification of educational goals, by a committee of college and university examiners. Handbook I: Cognitive domain.* New York: David McKay.

Boykin, A. W., & Noguera, P. (2011). *Creating the opportunity to learn: Moving from research to practice to close the achievement gap.* Alexandria, VA: ASCD.

Bradley, P. (2012). *Introduction to fake websites.* Retrieved from www.philb.com/fakesites.htm.

Browne, M. L., & Keeley, S. M. (2004). *Asking the right questions: A guide to critical thinking* (7th ed.). Upper Saddle River, NJ: Pearson Education.

Buck, G. A. (2002). Teaching discourses: Science teachers' responses to the voices of adolescent girls. *Learning Environments Research, 5,* 29–50.

Chaffee, J. (1988). *Thinking critically.* Boston: Houghton Mifflin.

Chaffee, J. (2006). *Thinking critically* (8th ed.). Wilmington, MA: Wadsworth.

Chartrand, J., Ishikawa, H., & Flander, S. (2009). *Critical thinking means business: Learn to apply and develop the new #1 workplace skill.* Upper Saddle River, NJ: Pearson Education. Retrieved from www.talentlens.com/en/downloads/whitepapers/Pearson _TalentLens_Critical_Thinking_Means_Business.pdf.

Civic Enterprises. (2006). *The silent epidemic: Perspectives of high school dropouts.* Washington, DC:Author. Retrieved from www.gatesfoundation.org/ unitedstates/Documents/ TheSilentEpidemic3-06FINAL.pdf.

The Conference Board, Inc., The Partnership for 21st Century Skills, Corporate Voices for Working Families, and Society for Human Resource Management. (2006). *Are they really ready to work? Employers' perspectives on the basic knowledge and applied skills of new entrants to the 21st century U.S. workforce.* New York: The Conference Board.

Costa, A. (Ed.). (2001). *Developing minds: A resource book for teaching thinking* (3rd ed.). Alexandria, VA: ASCD.

Day, M., Stobaugh, R., & Tassell, J. L. (2010, December). *Boosting the cognitive complexity of science assessments.* Presentation at the annual meeting of National Science Teachers Association Area Conference on Science Education, Nashville, TN.

Diamond, M., & Hopson, J. (1999). *Magic trees of the mind: How to nurture your child's intelligence, creativity, and healthy emotions from birth through adolescence.* New York: Penguin/Plume.

Dweck, C. (2006). *Mindset: The new psychology of success.* New York: Ballantine.

Facione, P. A. (1990a). *Technical report #1: Experimental validity and content validity.* Millbrae: California Academic Press. (ERIC 327 549).

Facione, P. A. (1990b). *Technical report #2: Factors predictive of CT skills.* East Lansing, MI: National Center for Research on Teacher Learning. (ERIC ED 327 550).

Facione, P. A. (2011). *Think critically.* Englewood Cliffs, NJ: Pearson Education.

Facione, P. A., & Facione, N.C. (1994). *Holistic critical thinking scoring rubric.* Millbrae: California Academic Press.

Facione, P. A., Facione, N. C., & Giancarlo, C. F. (1992). *The California critical thinking disposition inventory: Test manual.* Millbrae: California Academic Press.

Fleming, M., & Chambers, B. (1983). Teacher-made tests: Windows on the classroom. In W. E. Hathaway (Ed.), *Testing in the schools* (pp. 29–38). San Francisco: Jossey-Bass

Fogarty, R. (1997). *Brain compatible classrooms.* Arlington Heights, IL: Skylight Training.

Frisby, C. L. (1992). Construct validity and psychometric properties of the Cornell critical thinking test (Level Z): A contrasted group analysis. *Psychological Reports, 71,* 291–303.

Gabel, D., & National Science Teachers Association. (1994). *Handbook of research on science teaching and learning.* New York: Macmillan.

Goodlad, J. I. (2004). *A place called school* (2nd ed.). New York: McGraw-Hill.

Gronlund, N. E. (1981). *Measurement and evaluation in teaching.* New York: Macmillan.

Gronlund, N. E. (2006). *Assessment of student achievement* (8th ed.). Boston: Pearson Education.

Haladyna, T. M., Downing, S. M., & Rodriguez, M. C. (2002). A review of multiple-choice item-writing guidelines for classroom assessment. *Applied Measurement in Education, 15* (3), 309–334. doi: 10.1207/S15324818AME1503_5.

Hale, C. D., & Astolfi, D. M. (2011). *Measuring learning and performance: A primer* (2nd ed.). Retrieved from www.CharlesDennisHale.com.

Himmele, P., & Himmele, W. (2009). *The language-rich classroom: A research based framework for teaching English language learners.* Alexandria, VA: ASCD.

Insight Assessment. (n.d.). *Characteristics of critical thinkers.* Retrieved from www.insightassessment.com/.

Jacobs, S. S. (1995). Technical characteristics and some correlates of the California Critical Thinking Skills Test forms A and B. *Higher Education Research, 36,* 89–108.

Kentucky Department of Education. (2011). *Sample content for the Kentucky state assessment from the Stanford Achievement Test series.* Retrieved from www.education.ky.gov/KDE/Administrative+Resources/Testing+and+Reporting+/District+Support/Link+to+Released+Items/Sample+Assessment+Items+for+K-PREP.htm.

King, P. M., Wood, P. K., & Mines, R. A. (1990). Critical thinking among college and graduate students. *Review of Higher Education, 13* (2), 167–186.

Klaczynski, P. A. (2001). Analytic and heuristic processing influences on adolescent reasoning and decision making. *Child Development, 72*, 844–861.

Kurfiss, J. G. (1988). *Critical thinking: Theory, research, practice and possibilities. ASHE-ERIC Higher Education Report No. 2.* Washington, DC: Association for the Study of Higher Education.

Lemke, M., Sen, A., Pahlke, E., Partelow, L., Miller, D., Williams, T., Kastberg, D., & Jocelyn, L. (2004). *International outcomes of learning in mathematics literacy and problem solving: PISA 2003. Results from the U.S. perspective. (NCES 2005–003).* Washington, DC: U.S. Department of Education, National Center for Education Statistics.

Lyman, F. T. (1981). The responsive classroom discussion: The inclusion of all students. In A. Anderson (Ed.), *Mainstreaming digest* (pp. 109–113). College Park: University of Maryland Press.

Lynch, C. L., Wolcott, S. K., & Huber, G. E. (2001). *Steps for better thinking: A developmental problem solving process.* Retrieved from www.WolcottLynch.com.

Madaus, G. F., West, M. M., Harmon, M. C., Lomax, R. G., & Viator, K. A. (1992). *The influence of testing on teaching math and science in grades 4–12: Executive summary.* Chestnut Hill, MA: Boston College, Center for the Study of Testing, Evaluation, and Educational Policy.

Marzano, R. J. (2011). *The highly engaged classroom.* Bloomington, IN: Marzano Research Laboratories.

Marzano, R. J., Pickering, D. J., & Pollock, J. E. (2001). *Classroom instruction that works: Research-based strategies for increasing student achievement.* Alexandria, VA: ASCD.

Maxwell, M., Stobaugh, R., & Tassell, J. (2012). *CReaTe Framework.* Unpublished manuscript.

Mayer, R. E. (1999). *The promise of educational psychology: Learning in the content areas.* Upper Saddle River, NJ: Prentice Hall.

Mayer, R. E., & Wittrock, M. S. (1996). Problem-solving transfer. In D. C. Berliner and R. C. Calfee (Eds.), *Handbook of educational psychology* (pp. 47–62). New York: Macmillan.

Mehrens, W. A., & Lehmann, I. J. (1984). *Measurement and evaluation in education and psychology* (3rd ed.). New York: Holt, Rinehart & Winston.

MetLife. (2011). *The MetLife survey of the American teacher: Preparing students for college and careers.* Retrieved from www.metlife.com/about/corporate-profile/citizenship/metlife-foundation/metlife-survey-of-the-american-teacher.html?WT.mc_id=vu1101.

Michalko, M. (2011). *Creative thinkering.* Novato, CA: New World Library.

Mines, R. A., King, P. M., Hood, A. B., & Wood, P. K. (1990). Stages of intellectual development and associated critical thinking skills in college students. *Journal of College Student Development, 31*, 538–547.

Moore, B., & Stanley, T. (2010). *Critical thinking and formative assessments: Increasing the rigor in your classroom.* Larchmont, NY: Eye On Education.

National Center for Education Statistics. (2011). *The condition of education 2011.* Retrieved from http://nces.ed.gov/pubs2011/2011033_4.pdf.

National Center on Education and the Economy. (2008). *Tough choices or tough times: The report of the New Commission on the Skills of the American Workforce.* Washington, DC: Author.

National Governors Association Center for Best Practices, Council of Chief State School Officers. (2010a). *Common core state standards for English language arts & literacy in history/social studies, science, and technical subjects.* Washington, DC: Author. Retrieved from www.corestandards.org/assets/CCSSI_ELA%20Standards.pdf.

National Governors Association Center for Best Practices, Council of Chief State School Officers. (2010b). *Common core state standards for math.* Washington, DC: Author. Retrieved from www.corestandards.org/assets/CCSSI_Math%20Standards.pdf.

Nitko, A. J. (1983). *Educational tests and measurement: An introduction.* New York: Harcourt Brace Jovanovich.

Nitko, A. J., & Brookhart, S. M. (2011). *Educational assessment of students* (6th ed.). Upper Saddle River, NJ: Pearson Education.

Olson, K. (2009). *Wounded by school.* New York: Teachers College Press.

The Partnership for 21st Century Skills. (2011). *P21 Common Core toolkit: A guide to aligning the Common Core State Standards with the Framework for 21st Century Skills.* Washington, DC: Author.

Paul, R., & Elder, L. (2005). *A guide for educators to critical thinking competency standards.* Dillon Beach, CA: Foundation for Critical Thinking.

Paul, R., & Elder, L. (2007). *A guide for educators to critical thinking competency standards* (2nd ed.). Dillon Beach, CA: Foundation for Critical Thinking.

Paul, R., & Nosich, G. M. (1992). *A model for the national assessment of higher order thinking.* Santa Rosa, CA: Foundation for Critical Thinking.

Perkins, D. N. (1995). *Outsmarting IQ: The emerging science of learnable intelligence.* New York: Free Press.

Pogrow, S. (1990). Challenging at-risk learners: Finds from the HOTS program. *Phi Delta Kappan, 71* (5), 389–397.

Pogrow, S. (1994). Helping learners who "just don't understand." *Educational Leadership, 52* (3), 62–66.

Raths, J. (2002). Improving instruction. *Theory into Practice, 41* (4), 233–237.

Raudenbush, S. W., Rowan, B., & Cheong, Y. F. (1993). The pursuit of higher-order instructional goals in secondary schools: Class, teacher, and school influences. *American Educational Research Journal, 30*, 523–553.

Ray, B. (2012). *Design thinking: Lessons for the classroom.* Retrieved from www.edutopia.org/blog/design-thinking-betty-ray.

Reed, S. K. (2000). Problem solving. In A. E. Kazdin (Ed.), *Encyclopedia of psychology* (8th ed., pp. 71–75). Washington, DC: American Psychological Association.

Reich, R. (1989). *The resurgent liberal: And other unfashionable prophecies.* New York: Random House.

Ritchhart, R. (2002). *Intellectual character: What it is, why it matters and how to get it.* San Francisco: Jossey-Bass.

Ritchhart, R., Palmer, P., Church, M., & Tishman, S. (2006). *Thinking routines: Establishing patterns of thinking in the classroom.* Retrieved from www.pz.harvard.edu/research/AERA06Thinking Routines.pdf.

Ritchhart, R., & Perkins, D. (2008). Making thinking visible. *Educational Leadership, 65* (5), 57–61.

Rotherham, A. J., & Willingham, D. (2009). 21st century skills: The challenges ahead. *Educational Leadership, 67* (1), 16–21.

Schamel, D., & Ayres, M. P. (1992). The minds-on approach: Student creativity and personal involvement in undergraduate science laboratory. *Journal of College Science Teaching 21*, 226–229.

Shepard, L. (2001). The role of classroom assessment in teaching and learning. In V. Richardson (Ed.), *Handbook of research on teaching* (4th ed., pp. 1066–1101). Washington, DC: American Educational Research Association.

Shepard, L., Hammerness, K., Darling-Hammond, L., & Rust, F. (2005). Assessment. In L. Darling-Hammond & J. Bransford (Eds.), *Preparing teachers for a changing world: What teachers should learn and be able to do* (pp. 275–326). San Francisco: Jossey-Bass.

Siegler, R. S. (1998). *Children's thinking* (3rd ed.). Upper Saddle River, NJ: Prentice-Hall.

Silva, E. (2008). *Measuring skills for the 21st century*. Washington, DC: Education Sector Reports.

Stanley, S. (2006). *Creating an enquiring mind*. London: Continuum International.

Sternberg, R. J. (2008). *Cognitive psychology* (5th ed.). Belmont, CA: Thomson-Wadsworth.

Stiggins, R. J., Arter, J. A., Chappuis, J., & Chappuis, S. (2004). *Classroom assessment for student learning: Doing it right—using it well*. Portland, OR: Assessment Training Institute.

Stobaugh, R., Day, M. M., Tassell, J. L., & Blankenship, H. (2011). Boosting cognitive complexity in social studies assessments. *Social Studies and the Young Learner, 23*, 4–8.

Suskie, L. (2009). *Assessing student learning: A common sense guide* (2nd ed.). San Francisco: Jossey-Bass.

Swartz, R. J., & Parks, S. (1994). *Infusing critical and creative thinking into content instruction: A lesson design handbook for elementary grades*. Pacific Grove, CA: Critical Thinking Press and Software.

3M Corporation. (2001). *Polishing your presentation*. 3M Meeting Network Articles & Advice.

Tishman, S. (2001). Added value: A dispositional perspective on thinking. In A. L. Costa (Ed.), *Developing minds: A resource book for teaching thinking* (pp. 72–75). Alexandria, VA: ASCD.

Tomlinson, C. A., & Javius, E. L. (2012). Teach up for excellence. *Educational Leadership, 69* (5), 28–33.

Torff, B. (2005). Developmental changes in teachers' beliefs about critical-thinking activities. *Journal of Educational Psychology, 92*, 13–22.

Torff, B. (2006). Expert teachers' beliefs about critical-thinking activities. *Teacher Education Quarterly, 33*, 37–52.

Torff, B. (2008). Using the critical thinking belief appraisal to assess the rigor gap. *Learning Inquiry, 2*, 29–52.

Torff, B. (2011). Teacher beliefs shape learning for all students. *Phi Delta Kappan, 93* (3), 21–23.

Torres, R. M. (1993). *The cognitive ability and learning style of students enrolled in the College of Agriculture at The Ohio State University*. Unpublished doctoral dissertation. Columbus: Ohio State University

U.S. Department of Education, Office of Planning, Evaluation and Policy Development. (2010). *A blueprint for reform: The reauthorization of the Elementary and Secondary Education Act*. Washington, DC: Author.

Vosniadou, S. (2001). How children learn: Educational practices, series 7. *International Academy of Education*. Geneva, Switzerland: International Bureau of Education.

Retrieved from www.ibe.unesco.org/fileadmin/user_upload/archive/publica-tions/EducationalPracticesSeriesPdf/prac07e.pdf.

Wainer, H., & Kiely, G. (1987). Item clusters and computerized adaptive testing: A case for testlets. *Journal of Educational Measurement, 24*, 185–202.

Wenglinsky, H. (2000). *How teaching matters: Bringing the classroom back into discussion of teacher quality.* Princeton, NJ: Educational Testing Service.

Wenglinsky, H. (2002). The link between teacher classroom practices and student academic performance. *Education Policy Analysis Archives, 10*, 12. Retrieved from http://epaa.asu.edu/ojs/article/view/291.

Wenglinsky, H. (2003). Using large-scale research to gauge the impact of instructional practices on student reading comprehension: An exploratory study. *Education Policy Analysis Archives, 11*, 19. Retrieved from http://epaa.asu.edu/ojs/article/view/247.

Zohar, A., & Dori, J. (2003). Higher-order thinking and low-achieving students: Are they mutually exclusive? *Journal of the Learning Sciences, 12*, 145–182.